Spare Me 'The Talk'!
A Girl's Guide to Sex, Relationships, and Growing Up

"Although some parents will read the topic list and want to believe their daughters are too young for certain facts, we need to remember that research has shown that most parents underestimate their kids' readiness, interest, and need for sex education. Regarding sexuality and many other complex topics, children typically absorb what they are ready for and leave the rest for later. This book is your insurance policy that you are providing your daughter with the vital information she needs for sexual health and safety."

—Laura Kastner, Ph.D.,
author of *Getting to Calm* and *Wise-Minded Parenting*

"*Spare Me 'The Talk'!* provides adolescent girls a straightforward, thorough primer on sex that demystifies myths and provides answers for young women who are exploring sexual decision-making to help them make more informed choices. Today's girls are bombarded with mixed messages about sexuality; Jo Langford has created a resource that delivers information that adolescent girls can access over and over again."

—Julie Metzger R.N., M.N.,
cofounder of Great Conversations

"If you are worried about your daughter's ability to navigate the modern world of sexuality, offer her this book and give her what she needs to make great choices. Jo Langford tackles everything from periods and consent to sexting and being safe online. With a healthy dose of humor and practical, real-world advice and tips, this book will give teen girls a leg up when it comes to making decisions about sex."

—Amy Lang, M.A.,
author of *Dating Smarts: What Every Teen Needs to Know to Date, Relate, or Wait!*

Spare Me
'The Talk'!

A Girl's Guide to Sex,
Relationships, and Growing Up

JO LANGFORD, M.A.

ParentMap
'cause parenting is a trip!

Printed in the United States of America
Published by ParentMap
Distributed by Ingram Publisher Services

Cover photograph: Will Austin Photography, *willaustin.com*
Cover design: Amy Chinn

ISBN-13: 978-0-9904306-2-9

ParentMap dba Gracie Enterprises
7683 SE 27th St. PMB#190
Mercer Island, WA 98040
206-709-9026

ParentMap books are available at special discounts when purchased in bulk for premiums and sales promotions as well as for fundraisers or educational use. Place book orders at *parentmap.com* or 206-709-9026.

SFI® Certified Sourcing
www.sfiprogram.org
SFI-00453

SFI label applies to text stock

ACKNOWLEDGEMENTS

For my three most-importants: Amber, Xander, and 'Bella: You have taught me what it means to be strong, self-aware, and as much myself as I can be. I feel so fortunate that I am close to the man I always wanted to be. I am indebted to the three of you in more ways than I have words. Bells, you are already eight feet of personality stuffed into a three-foot sack. I hope this book helps you become even more powerful than you already are.

Thanks, also, to so many others who have been there for me: my family, friends (who also happen to be family), and colleagues (who also happen to be friends). Thank you all for the support, inspiration, conversation, patience, flames under my butt — and always, the palpable, palpable love.

Special thanks to the Super Powerful Task Force of Amazing Women, my smart and enthusiastic focus group, for the fantastic feedback — and, ultimately, the thumbs- up!

ParentMap is a Seattle-based resource for
award-winning parenting information.

parentmap.com

TABLE OF CONTENTS

INTRODUCTION

I am a therapist, a sex educator, and a dad. I've worked for decades to bring information (with humor) to underagers to increase their knowledge and self-confidence. I see this as an essential, proactive defense against the sometimes serious consequences that can accompany sexual activity.

We face an awful reality right now. Despite our resources, relatively high standard of living, and positive indices for life expectancy and education, the United States is one of the unhealthiest developed countries in the world with regard to sex and sexuality.

Whether you are already sexually active or are waiting until marriage, college, or this weekend, this book can help you protect yourself from unintended pregnancy and sexually transmitted infection.

If you are a teenage girl, consider this:
- Statistically, about 300,000 of you are going to get pregnant before you graduate from high school.[1]
- Approximately half of you are already sexually active in some way.[2]
- A quarter of you have already gotten a sexually transmitted infection (STI).[3]
- A third of you have received an aggressive solicitation from an online predator in the past year.[4]
- One out of every three of you has sent a nude picture to someone with your cell phone.[5]
- About a third of you will have been sexually assaulted in some way before your eighteenth birthday.[6]

Your parents spend a great deal of time worrying about sexual predators; these predators are on the front page of every paper, it seems. Websites and news channels are loaded with messages and warnings. While predators are real (and we'll talk about that in Chapters 17-20), it's easy for girls (and boys) to accidentally become their own worst enemy, especially where technology intersects with sexuality. Much of the sexual damage being done to you, as individuals and as a group, is preventable.

This book will help you to become your own best advocate by helping you prioritize your health, increase your level of self care and personal responsibility, and make healthy choices about your sexual expression and safety that will work for you.

Teenagers have been having sex since the beginning of time, and teenagers having sex doesn't scare me the way it scares some of your parents. Actually, that is not completely true — teenagers having sex scares me in the same way teenagers driving cars scares me.

You all know about defensive driving courses. The American National Standards Institute/American Society of Safety Engineers' *Safe Practices for Motor Vehicle Operations* defines defensive driving as "Driving to save lives, time, and money, in spite of the conditions around you and the actions of others."[7]

As an adult (and as a parent), I am a lot less worried when I know a teenager has learned to drive safely and is making an effort to prevent their driving from having a negative, life-changing impact on their own — and anyone else's — life.

My goal for this book is to serve as a "defensive sexuality course." It will help support and expand on "The Talk" — those discussions you may have had (or are having) with your parents about sex and sexuality. It offers a safe, private way to obtain the skills and information you need to make informed decisions. And it will give you the crucial tools with which to approach sex and sexuality with a sense of confidence and seriousness, having fun along the way while doing as little harm to yourselves and each other as possible; loving and relating in a way that "saves lives, time, and money, in spite of the conditions around you and the actions of others."

☛ *A special note about the values associated with this book:* I am a kinda crunchy, sorta groovy, West Coast, American, liberal, educated, secular, cisgender, bisexual, white dude. I am the dad of a powerful young woman, and a veteran sex educator, with decades of experience helping teenagers grapple with the many fun, fascinating, and sometimes frightening aspects of sex and sexuality. As such, I have a deep appreciation for the difficulty and confusion associated with puberty and adolescence — both for teens and for their parents.

My goal in writing this book is to share what I know from decades of working with young people, both boys and girls, and be as inclusive, thorough, and empowering as possible.

As such, I have written this book with the following in mind:

The Sex Bill of Rights

1 *Teens ought to be treated with respect.*

2 *Teens should be expected to be responsible for their own learning and experience, actions, and reactions.*

3 *Access to comprehensive sex education is every person's right.*

4 *Comprehensive sex education is an adult's responsibility to provide.*

5 *Vague terminology, sheepishness, and avoidance when talking about sex do not help anyone.*

6 *Fear and ignorance around sexuality cause harm.*

7 *All sex orientations and identities need to be acknowledged.*

8 *The realities and risks of teen sexual behavior need to be acknowledged.*

9 *Positive approaches that acknowledge the pleasurable aspects of sex, as well as the dangers and risks, work best when talking to teens.*

☛ *A special note for parents:* This book is the product of decades of experience as a professional sex educator. The pages that follow contain frank, open discussions and descriptions of the critical issues surrounding sex and sexuality that today's teenagers confront. It is widely acknowledged by experts that clear, complete information and education are our girls' single most effective defense against the risks and dangers surrounding teen sex, including pregnancy and diseases, from low-level to life-threatening.

I stand with the vast majority of child development and behavior experts — and decades of proven research — in holding that it is every teen girl's right to have access to unflinching and unbiased information about sex.

That said, you know your daughter best. For some teens, especially those fourteen and older, it may work best to simply give them this book and offer to discuss questions that come up. For younger girls, I recommend that you read this first and consider using it as a guide for discussion.

PART ONE
BIOLOGY AND IDENTITY

CHAPTER 1
The Girl Parts and the Boy Parts

Sexual health and mature sexual behavior are both very much dependent on having a good understanding of the human body — your own and your partner's. Some parts are reproductive, some are sexual, and some are both.

The 'Girl' Parts*
The female reproductive and sexual body parts are found within the body and on the outside. The exterior parts are collectively known as the vulva; these are the parts you can see.

*Of course, not everyone with these specific parts identify themselves as female, but the vast majority of those who identify as a girl or woman share these anatomical similarities. For more, see Chapter 4 on Sex, Gender, Identity, and Orientation (page 23).

The **vagina,** also called the birth canal, is near (but different from) the urethra, from which urine leaves the body. The vagina passes blood and substances during menstruation; produces fluids that cleanse and lubricate itself; and allows a pathway for sperm to reach the cervix (to cause pregnancy), and for the baby to leave the uterus (during birth). Vaginas are also commonly called "gynes" (pronounced "jines") or "vags" or sometimes "pussies," plus numerous other terms (but let's strive to use big-girl words).

The **cervix** is a small, mini-doughnut-shaped organ that connects the uterus and the back of the vagina.

The **hymen** is a thin piece of tissue that partially covers the opening of the vagina. This tissue often (but not always) becomes broken at some point in a woman's life. Some people believe the presence of a hymen means that particular woman is a virgin. The reality is that some women are born without hymens, some have hymens that are never truly broken, and many others have their hymens broken in ways other than sex.

The **mons** is the area above a woman's pubic bone — the part usually covered with hair. This provides protection for the pubic bone during intercourse, because otherwise? Ow. Two layers of lips, or **labia**, the majora (outer) and minora (inner), cover and protect the vagina.

The **clitoris** is a short shaft with a very sensitive tip, sometimes covered with a fold of skin called the clitoral hood. The clitoris is the only female organ that has the sole purpose of pleasure, and it plays an incredibly important part in arousal for women. It is located at the top of the opening of the vagina, above the urethra. For those of you who are sexually active with males (or plan to be someday), understand that some guys will a) not understand the clitoris's importance in sexual arousal for women, and b) may have difficulty locating it (as if "front and center" isn't obvious enough!). Do not be afraid to draw them a map if needed.

The **ovaries** are reproductive organs that produce ova (eggs). Eggs contain the female DNA and twenty-three chromosomes, which, if joined by the DNA and chromosomes of a sperm, create an embryo.

Fallopian tubes (also known as oviducts) are about 7- to 14-centimeter-long tubes that lead the egg from the ovaries into the **uterus** after ovulation (the release of the egg). Often, eggs are fertilized during this journey, creating the embryo. The uterus (or womb) is where the embryo attaches itself and eventually grows into a fetus during gestation.

The Gräfenberg spot, or **"G-spot,"** is a famously elusive female erogenous zone located inside the vagina. Erogenous zones are areas that, when stimulated, can lead to high levels of sexual arousal and powerful orgasms. The G-spot is typically found on the inner front wall of the vagina (behind the pubic bone). It's a small area of tissue that can become a bit swollen and feels very nice when it is massaged. Because it is on the front wall of the vagina, fingers are better for doing this than penises or other typically straight things. Some people, even some women, do not understand the G-spot, have any experience with it, or even believe it's a real thing. Others definitely do. I am one of them, but anatomical differences are typical and no one's body (or their relationship to it) is exactly the same as anyone else's. Your relationship to the G-spot is up to you.

The **breasts** of a female body contain the mammary glands, which make milk used to feed babies. When not feeding babies, female breast nipples are sensitive to the touch and can enhance sexual pleasure.

The 'Boy' Parts*
The **penis** is the main reproductive organ for male animals. It also serves as the male method of urination. Penises are also commonly called "dicks" or sometimes

"cocks," plus a ton of other terms (but again, let's strive to use big-girl words).

Of course, not everyone with these specific parts identify themselves as male, but the vast majority of those who identify as a boy or man share these anatomical similarities. For more, see Chapter Four on Sex, Gender, Identity, and Orientation (page 23).

The **scrotum** is the sac of skin and muscle that contains and (theoretically) protects the **testicles**. It is located between the penis and the anus. Testicles (or "balls") are composed of approximately 850 feet of tubules that produce the male hormone (testosterone) and make sperm. Like penises, testicles come in all different shapes and sizes.

Sperm are the male reproductive cells, and are composed of twenty-three chromosomes. Sperm are stored in the **epididymis** — a spongy layer of tubes located near the top of each testicle in which sperm grow and mature.

The **foreskin** is a retractable, double-layered fold of skin present on uncircumcised boys that covers and protects the **glans** of the penis when it is not erect. The glans is the sensitive "head" of the penis.

When a male is aroused and his penis becomes erect (hard), the foreskin slips back to expose the glans if he in uncircumcised (if he is circumcised, the glans is always exposed). When the penis head is stimulated and the penis gets hard (an erection, also called a "boner," a "hard-on," and loads of other terms, but ... big-girl words), the **vas deferens** transports sperm to the urethra. The **urethra** passes through the penis and opens to the outside to pass semen during ejaculation. This is also where urine leaves the body.

Along the way, several other glands work to add secretions to the sperm as it travels through the body. Sperm and these other substances make up **semen**, the milky-looking substance that helps sperm travel safely out of the penis to their next destination, and (sometimes) to join their DNA and chromosomes with that of a female egg to form an embryo.

The **prostate gland** is one of the glands that help create semen. The prostate is sometimes called the "male G-spot." It is located a couple of inches inside the anal canal and forward along the front wall of the rectum (toward the belly button). Stimulation of the prostate gland, through massage (with fingers) or anal intercourse (by a penis), can create sexual pleasure that is very different than the feelings caused when the head of the penis is stimulated. The **anus** is the opening of the rectum, which is also highly sensitive to touch and can provide sexual pleasure.

Note: Of course, girls also have anuses, but they do not have prostate glands.

CHAPTER 2
Puberty

Puberty is the process that signals the start of adolescence, when your child body begins to change into your adult body. It's the transition between childhood and adulthood.

Both male and female bodies will begin to take on a different shape during puberty, and each will develop stronger sexual characteristics. This happens at a fairly rapid pace, bringing with it new thoughts and feelings, as physical, emotional, and hormonal changes occur simultaneously. These changes do not take place on a strict or predictable timeline, which is one of the things that can make this time difficult for kids; the entire process can take anywhere from one to six years.

Puberty in females usually begins between the ages of eight and thirteen; for males, it's usually between the ages of nine and fourteen. Like the process itself, the age at which puberty starts can be different for everyone. This is not a big deal. We all end up in our adult bodies eventually.

When the body is going through puberty, the brain releases chemicals called hormones, which are responsible for all of the physical changes. These brain hormones stimulate the ovaries of girls to produce hormones called estrogen and progesterone, and the testicles of boys to produce testosterone.

Growth hormones are also stimulated and make the body grow larger. This can last for two or three years. Arms and legs get longer, and internal body organs get larger, and our overall body shape also changes. Girls usually become curvier during this time, gaining weight on their hips and experiencing an increase in overall body fat. This is when girls experience their first menstrual period. In females, breast development usually begins between the ages of ten and twelve, but again there is a lot of variation, just as their size and shape will vary when they are fully grown. In fact, many women's breasts are not symmetrical, and the left one may be just a bit different than the right. As girls mature sexually, their vaginas become lubricated when they are aroused, and they may also start having erotic dreams.

Boys will experience broader shoulders, stronger muscles, and darker, more developed genitals as well as pubic hair. The larynx lengthens, and the voice "breaks" or "cracks" as it becomes deeper. Boys generally begin producing semen between the ages of twelve and sixteen.[1] Spontaneous erections will start to occur, and possibly nocturnal emissions of sperm known as "wet dreams" (see page 52).

Another early sign of puberty for both sexes is hair growth. Hair grows under arms, on legs, and around genitals. Boys begin to grow hair on their faces and chests, and it might show up in a couple of other random places as well. As puberty progresses, it will become thicker, darker, and heavier.

☛ *A special note about pubic hair:* The hair on and around your genitals is called pubic hair. It's kind of important. Pubic hair provides a cushion of protection against both the friction from sexual activity and against certain bacteria. Pubic hair also is a sign that you are growing into your adult body, and it holds scents that can engage human brains in very sexy ways.

Like the hair on their heads, men and women do different things with the hair under the belts, from slight trimming to elaborate shapes to completely shaving with razor blades — or just letting it do whatever it wants to do.

Because there is very little pubic hair these days in mainstream, straight pornography, some girls feel weird about some of those options, and feel they need to shave their pubic hair completely off. This is simply not true.

Shaving your pubic hair with a blade can irritate the skin and leave microscopic open wounds. In a warm environment (such as your pants), these wounds make an excellent culture for infections such as MRSA (a type of staph bacteria), and can increase your vulnerability to herpes and other STIs. It also stings and makes you itch like a crazy person unless you keep shaving it. If you feel you absolutely *must* trim your pubic hair (or are simply curious), limit it to trimming the hedges a bit, but **do not put any razor blades near your genitals.**

Pubic hair is natural and nothing to feel weird about; our bodies put it there for a reason. And consider this: If the people who want to see you naked want you to look like a nine-year-old, you shouldn't let them see you naked!

The More Unfortunate Parts of Puberty
Acne is caused by the hormones produced during puberty. These are minor infections, also called pimples (or "zits"), and are caused when skin pores become clogged with dirt and oils.

The simplest way to keep your pores clean is to wash your skin regularly and thoroughly with a cleansing product — not necessarily soap, which can dry out your skin, causing it to produce more oils in response. Gel, cream, or lotion containing benzoyl peroxide, azelaic acid, or a topical antibiotic may also be applied directly to the skin. If you're concerned about your acne, it is worth visiting your doctor or a dermatologist for an expert opinion (and possibly, a prescription), but you may see improvement just by splashing clean water on your face a few times a day (maybe after washing your hands when you pee), and then drying with a clean towel.

Tips for preventing or improving acne:
- Try not to touch your face.
- Try not to wash your face too much or with harsh soap.
- Keep your hair clean and out of your face.
- Keep your sheets clean, especially pillowcases.
- Bathe at night, rather than in the morning. This helps prevent sleeping with your face pressed up against a pillowcase that has been marinating in your face's oil all night.
- Bathe in the morning, too. Because, why not?
- Eat a healthy, balanced diet.
- Don't squeeze blemishes. It just makes them angry.

Body odor is created when bacteria and sweat in certain body areas — specifically underarms, hair, and feet — become fragrant. Body odor (or "BO") is normal for everyone, but it can be more intense for teens. All humans have natural smells, many of which are pleasant and make us unique and attractive to other humans. We do not need to be ashamed of, or mask, our odors with chemicals and perfumes, but remember: Sharing the planet with other humans obligates us to make choices about how we want to present ourselves. In adolescence, hormones can make your natural (and usually pleasant) fragrances run amok. It's your choice whether to let your fragrances run wild or cloak them in body spray; either way, make the choice on purpose. Regular showering and carrying deodorant with you for touch-ups can help you manage the amount of personal scent you share with others.

☞ *A special note about BO:* There are going to be times when *you cannot smell yourself.* There are biological reasons for this, dating back to when we were cave people and needed to smell predators coming without being distracted by our own funk. Even though we have evolved in a lot of ways, our bodies still go through periods when we can't smell our own smells, which is why you are sometimes confused when your parents make that face when they open your bedroom door.

Besides BO and acne, puberty often brings a slew of more serious concerns, which can include depression, mood swings and energy fluctuations, risk taking, substance abuse, school problems, and problems brought on by stress. If you are experiencing any of these, don't hesitate to reach out for help, from a parent, your doctor, or a school nurse or counselor.

The timing, intensity, and duration of puberty are affected by genetics (your body shape and size, and your family history) and environment (nutrition, exercise, stress level, etc.). Everyone matures at his or her own pace, but ultimately, we all end up in the same general place.

Female Issues
Menstruation is the shedding of the blood and membrane that would have formed the nourishing home in the uterus for an embryo to grow into a fetus. Once you begin menstruation, each month that you do not get pregnant, the unused lining is sloughed off in the form of a bloody discharge. Menstruation (also called a "period") is considered the beginning of a woman's menstrual cycle. Periods are only part of a fairly complex physical and emotional cycle that happens every month for almost every woman between puberty and when menstruation stops at around age fifty (called "menopause").

The word "period" is one of many nicknames for menstruation. Some terms can imply shame or embarrassment, and some are code words that families have adopted to help with conversations. Here's a list of menstruation euphemisms that women have shared with me, which can help bring a little humor and empowerment to a process that (though it can help you feel grown up and connected to your body) can sometimes leave you feeling unsettled, awkward, and out of control.
   • Aunt Flo
   • The bleedies
   • Code red
   • Cousin from the south
   • The dot
   • Girly flu
   • Leak week
   • Little visitor
   • Monthlies
   • On the dot (or on the rag)
   • Red week
   • Special time
   • Surfing the crimson wave
   • That time of the month
   • Wetting the rag

Regardless of any teasing that may come from men or even other women, there is zero shame in the fact that you have a vagina, zero shame that you have hormones and body parts that make you a woman, and zero shame that your period is evidence of that. Be proud of yourself. Own it and call it whatever you want.

Your cycle, period, or whatever you decide to call it, is the time between the start of one bleeding period and the start of the next bleeding period. These cycles typically last twenty-eight days, but vary from woman to woman.

The actual **menstrual phase** (when the blood comes) can last from two days to about a week, depending on the woman. The discharge (or flow) can be light or heavy, can stop and start, and the thickness and color can change as well. It is more than just blood; there's other stuff, too, like unneeded or unused tissue and other fluids.

Ovulation (the release of an egg from the ovaries) occurs around day fourteen of the cycle. This is called the **proliferative phase,** when hormones trigger the release of an egg, which then begins to make its way toward the uterus. The egg moves down one of the fallopian tubes and reaches the uterus two to three days later.

You are typically most fertile (most likely to get pregnant) between day ten and day eighteen of your menstrual cycle, when the lining of your uterus starts to thicken to prepare for any fertilized eggs that may happen along. This is the **secretory (or luteal) phase,** which gets the uterus ready for the egg (should it happen to be fertilized by the sperm it's looking for). The entire ecosystem of your uterus shifts to accommodate a fertilized egg that might arrive, so it can implant on the wall of your uterus and start growing a baby.

If there is no fertilized egg, your uterus cleans house: The thickened lining of endometrium the uterus created to nourish the embryo gets flushed out (this is the actual period substance itself), and another cycle begins.

Typically, first periods occur around age twelve or thirteen. However, some girls can begin having periods as young as eight years old, and others may not start until they're sixteen.[1] Most first periods are a surprise, and can show up at any time. Once menstruation begins, it continues until **menopause** occurs (around the age of fifty), when a woman's monthly menstrual cycle changes and eventually ends.

Accidents happen on occasion. Having a change of clothes in your locker, desk, or the trunk of your car can be a good idea. Stains can be a bummer but are not a big deal. Typically, a mix of cold water and soap will take care of them, though for more stubborn stains, mixing in a bit of hydrogen peroxide, salt, or baking soda should do the trick.

Despite the presence of blood, there is no actual wound, although many women experience muscle pain, cramping, and discomfort. This can often be worse during adolescence. And your period does not just flow freely out of you as it would with an actual wound, either. Women can discharge between 4 and 12 tablespoons each cycle,[2] spread out over two to seven days during each cycle.

Myths and misunderstandings about menstruation abound. Regardless of what you've heard, these are the facts:

- You *can* have sex during a period (though some people choose not to).
- You *can* get pregnant during your periods. Use contraception.
- Periods typically last only a few days, but sperm can survive for as long as five days.
- Missing a period does *not* necessarily mean you are pregnant; stress, illness, and changes in weight and nutrition can all impact menstruation.
- Sharks and bears will *not* attack you just because you are menstruating.
- You *cannot* control the flow of your period (or "hold it in") with will power or physical effort (like you can with urine).

Some women have cycles that are "regular" — always roughly the same length, about the same flow — and some do not. Either way, it can be helpful to keep track your cycle, using a calendar or an app. Tracking your cycle can help you

- prepare for the physical and emotional effects that come with your period,
- track your fertility, knowing which days of the month you are most (or least) likely to get pregnant,
- notice any changes or issues that may require a doctors' visit,
- notice any missed or late periods as soon as possible,
- get early warning — which can be important if you are one of those women whose periods can be particularly difficult, and may require extra rest and self care, or avoidance of certain things (or people!).

Premenstrual syndrome (PMS) and premenstrual tension (PMT) include a range of symptoms that happen during the time between ovulation and menstruation. Most women (approximately 85 percent[3]) experience some symptoms of PMS/PMT. These symptoms are usually predictable and most often occur in the days just before a period.

The most common symptoms include

- irritability, tension, and mood swings
- cramps
- abdominal pains
- depression, crankiness, and sadness
- difficulty concentrating
- sore breasts

- weight gain (because the body is retaining water)
- fatigue
- headaches
- cravings for specific foods
- other medical issues, such as headaches, asthma, or allergies

Things that can help:
- Comfy clothing. A go-to "uniform" can be both comfortable and comforting.
- Mind your cravings. Sugar, salt, and caffeine (although they can sound like a great idea in the moment) can exacerbate some PMS/PMT symptoms, making symptoms such as fatigue, bloating, and headaches worse. Try to eat them sparingly; or better yet, stick to protein and fresh fruits and veggies.
- Good chocolate (not milk chocolate!). Chocolate containing sixty percent or more of cacao can improve your mood, reduce cravings and stress, and give you a dose of magnesium, which can help with cramping.
- Water.
- Water.
- Water.
- Exercise. Keeping your body moving (even if you feel like just lying on the floor) can release endorphins, which can improve your mood and provide a nice distraction.
- Pain relief. Ibuprofen or acetaminophen can reduce muscle soreness caused by cramping. So can having an orgasm (either with a partner or just by yourself).
- Heat. Heating pads, blankets, oversize mugs of tea, and even small animals to cuddle with can help keep your abdomen warm and soothed.
- Be nice to yourself. If lying around in a giant sweater with your hair in a ponytail, binge-watching mid-'90s teen dramas does it for you, then do it! As a woman, you can spend the equivalent of six years of your life menstruating[4]. Use your periods as time to do something nice for yourself.

Feminine hygiene products. Although periods typically may only mean a few ounces of fluid discharged per day, you still need to manage it, and there are several ways to do this.

There are loads of choices, and what works for you may be influenced and determined by your environment, *the* environment, your lifestyle, your bank account, and/or other factors. Choose whichever product (or products) work best for you. Some of the most common of these products are listed below.

Pads are great for those of you who are still getting used to having a period, have heavier flows, and for while you are sleeping. There are tons of different kinds and sizes, with different shapes and superpowers, but most have an adhesive backing (like a Band-Aid does) that help them stick to your underwear and stay in place. The other side typically contains a blend of soft, absorbent synthetic and natural fibers, which collect the discharge and (hopefully) contain leaks.

Some women prefer organic, unbleached, natural cotton pads, but they may be sacrificing some absorbency. Some women may prefer the worry-free absorbency, and even the pleasant fragrances, of some of the artificial fibers of others, though they may risk irritation from synthetics, perfumes, or plastics. Washable, reusable pads have come a long way, technologically speaking. These can be quite a bit less expensive in the long run, and are arguably better for the environment, although they require regular laundering.

Tampons are small, cottony, absorbent pods that you can insert into your vagina during your period. The material soaks up discharge before it exits your body. Some women find them more comfortable than pads, and say they are easier and more manageable for events and activities such as sports. As with pads, there is a range of types and fibers available, from synthetic-based fibers combined with cotton to unbleached, natural fibers.

Menstrual cups are exactly what they sound like: thumb-size, rubber or silicone cups that can be inserted into your vagina where they literally catch your menstrual flow. The cups can be removed, emptied, and reused. There are also disposable cups available, but the rubber ones can last a long time with proper care and cleaning between uses.

Natural sea sponges are actual — but no longer living! — sea creatures that are soft, surprisingly absorbent, easy to clean, and reusable. Moistened with warm water, the (store-bought) sponges are inserted into the vagina to collect fluid. These sponges don't last forever and can be a bit messy to remove, but they are low cost and easy on the environment, making them the eco-grooviest of options.

Regardless of which you choose, all products should be handled with clean hands and changed regularly. And keep extras in your car, bag, locker at school, and/or desk at work — at one point or another, you're bound to be glad you did.

🐖 *A special note about toxic shock syndrome:* Toxic shock syndrome (TSS) is a rare but dangerous illness associated with the use of superabsorbent tampons while menstruating. TSS is caused by bacteria that release toxins into the body, and can be guarded against by using lower-absorbency tampons, changing them regularly, and not wearing them at night. As awareness has grown over the past couple of decades, the incidence of tampon-caused TSS has declined. Today, it is relatively rare, but when it happens, it is quite serious and requires immediate medical assistance. Possible signs and symptoms of toxic shock syndrome include

- a sudden high fever
- low blood pressure (hypotension)
- vomiting or diarrhea
- a rash that resembles a sunburn, particularly on your palms and soles of your feet
- confusion
- muscle aches
- redness of your eyes, mouth, and throat
- seizures
- headaches

☞ *A special note about douches:* As with everything else, don't fall for ads and products that make you feel self-conscious, particularly if they are trying to make you feel self-conscious about weird vaginal smells. Some advertisers may try to get you to worry that someone passing you on the sidewalk or in the hallway is going to notice an odor. It's a vagina, not a fast-food restaurant you can smell a block away! As long as you are doing basic and regular hygiene, maintaining a healthy diet, and being generally nice to your swimsuit area, odor should not be an issue.

Vaginas have a natural odor, which is healthy and can even be pleasant. Perfumes and other artificial substances can be bad for the somewhat fragile ecosystem that is your vagina, so avoid products and washes (called douches) that introduce fragrances or other chemicals to your vagina. Douches are an outdated and generally unnecessary product that women were encouraged to use, back in the day when they were *not* encouraged to do things like speak up for themselves, use birth control, or get jobs.

Douching can deplete the mucus, moisture, and good bacteria that make for healthy vaginas. There is also evidence that douching can contribute to a number of health issues, including cervical cancer, pelvic inflammatory disease, and sexually transmitted infections[5]. In general, unless prescribed by a doctor, there is no reason you should ever douche your vagina.

Douches are either: a) a preparation choice that some people make prior to engaging in anal sex (for sanitary reasons); or b) obnoxious guys who treat women like crap because they think they are more popular, desirable, or classier than they actually are.

☛ ***A special note about guys and periods:*** It's a good thing for males to understand the impact that biology has on the women in their lives, but a lot of guys just don't get it. Your dad, brothers, friends, boyfriends, roommates, or, someday, sons may need some coaching about what you go through and what you need during this time. The more information they get, the more likely they are to

- show understanding and compassion,
- reject ridiculous stereotypes about girls who are having their period,
- refuse to tease or shame girls, or hold their periods against them,
- be prepared for the emotional or behavioral changes experienced by the women in their lives.

At some point, a guy may ask you, "Are you having your period?" Strive to gently remind him that this is not an OK question to ask. Try to go easy on them; it can be very hard for a guy to wrap his brain around the idea of bleeding for days from a reproductive organ — without dying. Many guys probably wouldn't be able to handle it!

Breast size. American culture places a strange emphasis on breast size, and mixed messages are rampant. Although breast augmentation is one of the most popular cosmetic surgeries in the United States, the U.S. Justice Department spent $8,000 in 2002 on curtains to hide the breasts of a topless Lady Justice statue from cameras during press conferences.[6]

You can be treated differently if you have particularly large or especially small breasts (also known as "boobs"). Large breasts are painful and awkward to deal with. Some girls with smaller breasts may feel inadequate. Women are inundated for most of their lives with idealized or unrealistic images about breast size. Not only are you pressured by men, but sometimes by other women as well! Breast implants make some women feel more attractive, but such implants also shorten their life spans — and make them statistically three times more likely to kill themselves.[7]

It is important that you to strive to be comfortable with and proud of your body. Take care of it and keep it as healthy as possible, and find the self-esteem to rise above the expectations and judgments of others. We all need to remember that the two most important things about boobs — the ability to breastfeed and the risk of breast cancer — are completely unrelated to size.

Breast self-exams. Women of all ages are encouraged to perform breast self-exams at least once a month, according to Johns Hopkins Medical Center, because 40 percent of diagnosed breast cancers are detected by women who feel a lump.[8] While a mammogram (an X-ray of your breasts) can help to detect cancer before you can feel a lump, regular breast self-exams help you become familiar with how your breasts look and feel, making it more likely you'll notice any changes.

It's especially important to examine yourself regularly if breast cancer runs in your family. Breast self-exams can be done in the shower, in front of a mirror, or lying down on your back. During the monthly exam, you will be methodically and carefully feeling your breasts and nipples, looking for any lumps, bumps, or changes since the last time you checked. You can find step-by-step instructions, apps, and videos in various places online (try *nationalbreastcancer.org/breast-self-exam*); basically you will be looking for

- painless or painful lumps or knots
- changes in shape or size
- differences in shape (between the left and right; remember that few women have an exactly matching pair)
- dimples or tucks that were not previously there
- redness or scaliness, like dry skin

You cannot rely only on breast self-exams to be sure you are cancer free. Early detection is important to save lives, so combine your regular self-exams with regular medical care and appropriate guideline-recommended mammography.

If you find a lump — don't panic. Eight out of ten lumps are not cancerous, but you should make an appointment with your doctor and get it checked.[9]

Gynecology. Speaking of doctors, an OB-GYN (each letter is pronounced: "O-B-G-Y-N") doctor is a specialist in obstetrics and gynecology. Obstetrics is the branch of medicine that deals with pregnancy and childbirth; gynecology deals with the female reproductive system. The American College of Obstetricians and Gynecologists recommends that young women have their first visit with an OB-GYN between the ages of thirteen and fifteen.[10]

OB-GYNs are not the only medical professionals who provide health care for young women. Many other professionals are also trained in women's health, including family nurse practitioners, advanced practice nurse practitioners, certified nurse midwives, and licensed midwives. Your pediatrician may also be an option for you as long as you are legally a minor.

You may feel a bit uncomfortable or embarrassed at the prospect of visiting your doctor, but it's super important for your sexual health — especially if you have a family history of reproductive health issues, are sexually active, or are pregnant. You can choose whether to visit a male or a female OB-GYN.

Appointments usually involve
- a physical examination (much like ones you have likely gotten all your life)
- conversations about your body, habits, and general health
- a breast exam, to look for lumps, cysts, or other concerning changes as you grow and develop
- an external examination of your vulva, again to screen for any concerns

Once you are in your twenties (and/or when you become sexually active), your gynecological exams will expand to include
- An internal examination of your vagina. Your doctor will use fingers and a tool called a speculum to gently hold open your vagina for a visual examination, as well as palpate (feel) your ovaries and uterus. This is not usually painful, though some women feel pressure or discomfort.
- A pap smear. This is the swabbing of cells from your cervix to screen for strains of human papillomavirus (HPV) and forms of cancer not covered by the vaccine (which you can get from your medical provider if you haven't already; see page 78).

It can help to accompany a relative or friend on one of their gynecological exams before you have your first one, to get an idea of the process. It's also totally OK to bring someone with you, such as your mother or a female friend (although dads and boyfriends can also be supportive).

☞ *A special note about privacy:* As you get older, your health care becomes your own responsibility (just like your other basic hygiene), and it is totally OK to move your parents into a resource category (rather than a companion). No one will make you have a parent in the room during doctor visits if you do not want it.

If your parents do accompany you, your doctor will probably ask them to leave the room while you talk anyway, because it is very important for you to be able to be honest and open with your doctor about things you might not want to talk about with your mom (or even BFF) in the room. If your doctor does not automatically ask them to wait outside (or ask for your preference), it is your right to ask for privacy during your exams. Not being honest with your doctor can affect your sexual health as well as the health of others. If your doctor does ask that a parent or a support person wait outside, and you are uncomfortable being alone for any reason, you can always ask for a nurse or technician to join you.

Gynecological exams are safe and totally confidential, so it is OK to ask any questions and speak openly and honestly about your body, sexual activity, substance use, and other issues. Your health care and your sexual and mental health are protected by your relationship with your doctor. Doctors cannot legally share any of your personal information with your parents, unless they have a reason to believe your health or life (or someone else's) is in danger.

☛ *A special note about parents:* Not everyone has the luxury of having caring parents (who know what they are talking about) as a resource. But unless you have clear evidence to the contrary, such as emotional or physical abuse in your home, trust that your parents have your best interests in mind (even if you disagree about values). You may not want to go to your parents with questions about sex and sexuality, and that is OK. But it is *not* OK for you to avoid asking those questions. If you can't or won't ask your parents, ask your doctor.

But the great thing about parents is that they love you — and they're more readily available. Of course, some parents are better at this type of talk than others. Your parents may not have been able to talk with *their* parents about this stuff, and they may need your help in the form of patience and prompting. If it gets too awkward, talk about how awkward it's getting — and then ask your parents to help you find someone else to talk to. Sometimes, it's a drag raising parents, but they've stuck with you through lots of stressful and awkward things, like driving and pooping.

And if you need to keep all of this very separate from your parents, fine: You can also get the care and answers you need through community-based clinics (such as Planned Parenthood).

Yeast infections (also known as candidiasis or thrush) are fungal infections of the vagina. Candida yeasts are usually present in most women, but are kept in check by other naturally occurring bacteria. However, external irritants (such as some soaps, douches, glycerin-based lubricants, sex, sweatiness, etc.) or internal disturbances (caused by things such as medications, contraceptives, or pregnancy) can mess with the delicate pH balance of the vagina, and an overgrowth of yeast can result.

Yeast can also be transmitted between people by direct contact, and so can be considered a sexually transmitted infection. A yeast-infected person can infect other partners, then get re-infected the next time they have sex with them. Indirect transmission may also occur as the fungi can survive in bed linens, towels, and articles of clothing for long periods of time.

Most medical descriptions compare the discharge to ricotta cheese and the scent to baked bread. There is an intense itching, burning sensation, localized in the vagina and vulva, which can become so painful it can become hard to walk. Yeast infections are commonly treated with antimycotics (antifungal drugs).

Urinary tract infections, or **UTIs** (also called cystitis or bladder infections), are due to bacteria infecting the urethra or bladder, rather than yeast. Boys can get UTIs as well, but these infections are considered mostly a girl thing because women's urinary tracts are shorter, and in closer proximity to things such as vaginas and anuses.

UTIs can have you feeling as if you have to pee constantly, and it may be painful or smelly when you do. Some people are more susceptible to UTIs than others, though everyone can take steps to prevent them:
• Pee when you need to pee (don't hold it too long).
• Remove tampons before peeing.
• Pee after sexual contact.
• Always wipe front to back when you pee.
• Stay hydrated by drinking water.
• Drink cranberry juice, which contains natural antibacterial substances.
• Don't introduce soaps, deodorants, or other chemicals to your vagina.
• Avoid sexual activity.

Urinary tract infections are not likely to go away without medical treatment, which can include antibiotics and pain relievers. Leaving urinary or bladder infections untreated can lead to serious kidney problems, so it's important to get an appointment with your doctor as soon as you think you may have a UTI. Besides, they hurt! If you can't see your doctor right away, talk to your pharmacist about over-the-counter pain relief in the meantime.

To help protect against yeast and urinary tract infections, do not share unwashed towels, clothing (especially underwear), or bed linens. Good hygiene is always a good thing, and in this case, it means keeping yourself clean and dry by bathing regularly and wearing clean, loose cotton underwear.

Jock itch, scientifically known as tinea cruris, is a fungal infection of the groin region. Jock itch is not just for boys; it can affect anyone who sweats a lot. This infection thrives in warm, damp environments — such as tight, sweaty, or rubbing clothing, which allows the fungus to grow out of control. Fungus from other parts of the body (such as tinea pedis or "athlete's foot") can also contribute to jock itch, which causes an itching or burning sensation in the genital and surrounding areas. Affected areas may appear red or brown, with flaking, peeling, or cracking skin. Mycosis infections, another name for fungal infections, are commonly treated with antimycotics. Indirect transmission may also occur, as the fungi can survive on bed linens, towels, and articles of clothing for long periods of time.

General signs of a less than healthy gyne:
- excessive vaginal dryness (until you are older)
- excessive discharge, regardless of smell or color
- smells while urinating (or odors are not taken care of by regular bathing)
- itching and burning (especially while urinating)
- blood (unless you are having your period or especially after intercourse)

Note: If you are worried about any health issue, but especially one that has to do with your swimsuit area, **go to the doctor.** Google and Bing will give you some good, basic information — and then will start to freak you out. The Internet (like this book) is *no* replacement for a physician!

Male Issues

Penis size. Just like women and their breasts, a lot of guys can become obsessed with their penises — its habits, its behaviors, and its size. A penis is the very first toy a guy gets, and they play with them all their lives. They makes jokes about them, have the luxury of peeing while standing because of them, and most men will protect their penises with their lives.

This special relationship, though, can also come with a price, and that price is called "boner shame." Most people do not have a realistic idea of how big the average penis is — guys included, because most of the other erect penises most guys have seen (besides their own) have been in porn. There is a reason that a lot of these guys are in the porn business, and it is usually not their acting ability. Also, the perspective with which guys see their own penises is limited, and nothing like what anyone else sees. Even when they take pictures of them with their phones, it is a distorted image.

P.S. When they send those pictures to you, tell them to stop.

Regardless of what they look like when they're flaccid (soft), nine out of ten penises are basically the same length when erect (hard). The average penis is about 5.6 inches when erect.[11]

To make things even more complicated, there are two different kinds of penises: "growers" and "showers." A shower is long when it is soft, and does not increase much in length as it becomes erect. A grower is shorter when soft, and increases much more (sometimes doubling or tripling in length) as it gets erect. It is estimated that almost 80 percent of men are growers.[12] But whether grower or shower, most penises are still about 5 inches when erect. In fact, only five men out of every 100 have an erection longer than 6 inches.[13]

The typical vagina of a woman is only about 3 inches long when not sexually excited and, when it is, it is usually only an inch or so longer.[14] There is no "normal" size when it comes to penis size or shape. Nor is there a normal size when it comes to vagina size or shape. In fact, it has been found that the nerve placement and pathways can be completely different for every woman. The bottom line is: For most people, satisfying sexual experiences have very little to do with the size or shape of the organs, and a lot more to do with what (and whom) you do with it.

Circumcision is a surgical procedure in which the foreskin is cut off or removed from a penis. In Jewish culture, it is a religious ritual, symbolizing an outward sign of a compact with God. This procedure is most often done when boys are infants.

According to the Centers for Disease Control and Prevention (CDC), approximately half of all baby boys released from hospitals have their foreskins intact. Circumcision is relatively rare worldwide (approximately 16 percent in Britain[15]), and has become less popular in recent years, as more and more people have come to see circumcision as a painful and unnecessary surgery. If and when you become sexually active with a guy, there is almost a 50/50 chance that he will be circumcised.

Blue balls refer to a localized pain in the testicles that can happen if blood flow to the penis (which is what makes it get hard) lasts too long. The ache
- is relatively minor,
- is experienced by most guys at some point,
- causes no damage,
- will eventually go away by itself (or can be taken care of by ejaculating).

Some guys may use this pain to try to persuade others to have sex with them. Don't fall for it; if it's that bad, he can take care of it himself, if you know what I mean. (He knows what I mean.)

Body Image
Body image is the way we see ourselves in our minds and in our mirrors, and the way we think and feel about what we see.

A negative body image is a perception of our self — whether true or distorted — that causes shame, anxiety, or self-consciousness, or that interferes with our relationships with ourselves and other people.

A positive body image is an acceptance of your body, and a feeling of comfort and confidence about it. A positive body image also may or may not be accurate. Ideally, we are seeing the parts of our bodies mostly as they really are.

People have put time, energy, money, and other valuable resources into physical appearance since the beginning of time. Most of us are more concerned with our appearance than we'd care to admit. Advances in medicine and technology as well as media have caused such concern to sometimes shift into obsession.

Everyone experiences body dissatisfaction at some point. What you see and how you react to your reflection in a mirror will vary according to your sex, age, environment, sexual orientation, peer culture, societal views in general, whether you have a partner or are single, what kind of relationship you're in, what kind of childhood you had, whether you take part in sports, what phase of the menstrual cycle you're in — even what you media you consume, through television, magazines, and the Internet.

Warning signs of negative body image include
- low self-esteem
- negative self-talk
- a strong need to fit in
- depression
- unrealistic body standards
- excessive exercise
- disordered eating habits

The two biggest eating disorders are anorexia (starvation) and bulimia (binging and purging). More than 1 million Americans have eating disorders; the vast majority of them are girls.[16] Many eating disorders cause damage to your heart, throat, metabolism, and bowels, and 10 percent of people with eating disorders die within ten years.[17]

It is extremely important to speak to your doctor if you have concerns about your body, if you find yourself not eating for long periods of time, or if you regularly make yourself throw up. It is difficult to develop anorexia, bulimia, or other disordered eating habits if you have a healthy level of self-esteem and a healthy body image. A healthy body image helps us experience — but not internalize — society's socially sanctioned standards of beauty. In our society, women are judged more often and more critically on their appearance than men. American standards of female beauty are higher and less flexible than they are for men.

Have you ever seen the hot husband/frumpy wife sitcom? Of course you haven't! Has any major news anchor ever cared or commented on what outfit or shoes a male senator is wearing? The buffness of Michelle Obama's arms is an almost constant topic of conversation in women's magazines — but not Barack's. You can find out how much Angelina Jolie weighs by standing in any grocery store checkout line — but not Brad.

But don't be fooled into thinking that eating disorders do not have an impact on men as well; statistically, 10 percent of eating-disordered people are male.[18] The boy versions of these issues are (only somewhat jokingly) referred to as "manorexia" or "boylimia," but they do exist and are more dominant in people who are teased about their bodies as children, those who are overweight, and athletes.

Here are things you can do to create and maintain a positive body image:
- Focus on associating with people who are trustworthy and genuinely concerned about your health.
- Give compliments to others, and learn how to take them.
- Avoid perfectionism.
- Exercise to relieve stress and stay healthy.
- Get involved in groups, clubs, teams, and sports. This exposes you to a diversity of people.
- Focus on things you do well.
- Help others. This has an even greater impact on positive self-worth than giving compliments.
- Remember that everybody is different, including you, and be proud of that.

If you can't find a way to do the steps listed above on your own, consider finding a therapist to help.

Basic hygiene is important for positive self-image and a healthy relationship with your own body. Hygiene refers to the behaviors and routines we use to keep our bodies clean and healthy, such as bathing, brushing and flossing, and wearing clean underwear and socks.

Healthy people have some sort of daily hygiene ritual or routine. At the minimum, this should include a clean body, clean teeth, and clean clothes. For most girls, deodorant, and some kind of intentional effort with their hair are also part of daily hygiene. Trimming your nails, choosing whether or not to use perfume or product in your hair, and deciding whether or not to shave your underarms or legs are also part of the many things that make up one's personal hygiene.

Your hygiene routine will be as individual as you — and a reflection of the time and care you take to keep your body at its best.

CHAPTER 4

Sex, Gender, Identity, and Orientation

Sex and gender

Sex and gender are different things. Your **sex** is associated with your physical parts and biological status as male or female. It is a reproductive category, referring to physical attributes such as sex chromosomes, gonads (testicles and ovaries), hormones, internal reproductive structures, and genitalia — the boy parts and the girl parts. It's where you are on the spectrum of male to female.

Your **gender** (where you are on the spectrum of masculine to feminine) is a social phenomenon having to do with societal cultural expectations about how a person of a given sex "ought" to behave. The term "gender" is often used to refer to the ways that people act, interact, or feel about themselves — how "guy-like" or "chick-like" you are — and it has nothing to do with what kind of genitals you have. Instead, it has to do with the time period, family, culture, and geographical location in which you live. It can be changed depending on the situation, time, and place. Masculinity and femininity are cultural inventions that refer to where you are on the spectrum of masculine to feminine.

Sexual Identity and the Continuum

Sexual identity is your identity with respect to the plumbing with which you were born (or acquire later through surgery) — the physical parts, including the hormones, the chromosomes, and other body characteristics associated with males and females. An **intersex** person is on the continuum and
• may have both male and female biological characteristics;
• may be chromosomally (internally) one sex, while physically (externally) another;
• may have biological sex characteristics that cannot be classified as either male or female.

The word "hermaphrodite" has been used to refer to people with both male and female sexual organs, but this term is misleading, stigmatizing, and should never be used. There are no actual human hermaphrodites. The preferred term for someone with atypical combinations of features that are usually considered male or female is intersex.

Gender Identity and the Spectrum

Gender identity refers to one's sense of oneself as a man, a woman, both, or neither. Trans(gender) or cis(gender) can be descriptors of this phenomenon.

Transgender is an umbrella term used to describe people whose gender identity (sense of themselves as male or female) or gender expression may differ from the body shape and parts they were born with. Examples of this include a girl born with boy parts, or someone who feels like a boy on the inside, but was born with a girl's body.

The opposite of this is **cisgender**. This is when your sense of yourself as a male or a female matches your body's biology.

Other gender identities on the spectrum include **genderqueer** and **gender fluid;** these are people who may think of themselves as
  • being a third sex — both male and female;
  • moving back and forth between genders;
  • falling completely outside the gender binary as genderless (or agender), neither male nor female, and/or rejecting the idea of a gender binary.

Your gender identity is connected to, but not dependent on, your sexual identity.

Transsexuals are transgender people who engage in hormone therapies and surgical procedures (called gender reassignment or gender confirmation surgeries) to live as members of the gender opposite to the sex they were born as. Biological females who wish to live and be recognized as men are called female-to-male (FTM) transsexuals, or transsexual men. Biological males who wish to live and be recognized as women are called male-to-female (MTF) transsexuals, or transsexual women.

Gender identity and sexual identity are different; transgender people can be gay, straight, or bisexual; masculine, feminine, or androgynous. You can't tell if someone is trans just by their appearance. It's important to remember that not everyone whose appearance or behavior is gender-atypical identifies as transgender.

There are now approximately 700,000 trans people in the U.S.[1], and we are evolving a new understanding that there is no true gender binary — meaning that there are more than just two distinct genders, male and female. In reality, there are many shades of gray in between.

☛*A special note about vocabulary:* A new vocabulary is emerging to solve challenges around fluid, mixed, and separate identities. It is socially acceptable (in fact, encouraged) to ask people, "What pronouns do you prefer?"

The answers might go beyond the expected "he/him/his," "she/her/hers," or "they/them/theirs."

Alternative pronouns are becoming increasingly common, especially on college campuses, to reflect the growing diversity of sexual identities. These days, you may hear:

"ey/em/eirs," "ze/hir/hirs," or "ze/zir/zirs." As in:

"Ey is going to the movies. I am going with em. We are taking eir car."

Or

"Ze is going to the movies. I am going with zir. We are taking zir car."

Schools, including day cares, are now moving toward more open pronoun policies in light of this new hyper-individuation of identity, and Facebook profiles offer more than 50 different gender options to choose from.

There are dozens of variations on this dynamic, important, and confusing concept.

It is important to understand that **misgendering** isn't seen as a typo anymore; it's seen as a refusal to offer another person basic, ground-level dignity. Once you know someone's preference, it is polite to do your best to respect that person's choices.

In all of the above cases, pronouns should not be based on the shape of one's genitals, the clothes one wears, or any other outside detail, but instead on what one prefers to be called. When in doubt, just ask.

Transvestites, or cross-dressers, wear clothing typical of the opposite sex to varying degrees. Some cross-dress to express cross-gender feelings, some do it for fun, some for emotional comfort or sexual arousal. The majority of cross-dressers are straight males. Transvestites may or may not also identify as transgender.

Drag queens (males) and **drag kings** (females) live part-time as members of the other sex, primarily as performers. The majority of drag performers identify as gay or lesbian, and may or may not identify as transgender.

Identity and expression (or orientation) are also different things.

Sexual Expression and the Spectrum
Sexual expression and **sexual orientation** refer to which sex you choose to be sexual with, and that sex's relationship to your own. Sexual orientation refers to one's sexual attraction to men, women, both, or neither; that is, where you are on the spectrum of gay to straight, with bisexual somewhere in the middle.

Heterosexuality

Heterosexuality is physical and/or emotional attraction to people of the opposite sex; when a man and a woman have a romantic or sexual relationship. Heterosexuality is also called "being straight." This is a strange term that implies that not only is heterosexuality the norm for most people (which is true), but also that anyone who is not heterosexual is "bent" (which is *not* true).

Heterosexuality is the visibly predominant behavior with regard to sex, and the primary way that our species can reproduce new generations. This doesn't make it better or more "normal" than any other orientation.

Homosexuality

Homosexuality is the romantic or sexual attraction to someone of the same sex. Though the word "gay" is used in general to describe this, gay typically refers to a male who is attracted to another male, and "lesbian" is the preferred term for a female who is attracted to another female.

Gay myths:
- You can tell who is gay by the way they act.
- Gay people want to be the opposite sex.
- Only gay people get HIV/AIDS.
- Gay people are more likely to become child molesters.
- If someone is abused by someone of the same sex, they can become gay.
- Gay is contagious.
- Gay people choose to be gay.
- Gay people can choose not to be gay.
- Having fantasies about someone of the same sex means you are gay.
- Sexual contact with someone of the same sex makes you gay.

Same-sex sex is a phenomenon that has been observed in hundreds of species[2]; mammals and sea life, including lions, dolphins, and killer whales; even birds and worms. In fact, no species has been found in which homosexual behavior does not exist (with the exception of species that never have sex at all or that are hermaphroditic).

The term **GLBTQ** stands for gay, lesbian, bisexual, transgender, and queer (meaning "not straight") or questioning (meaning "I haven't made up my mind yet"). **LGBTQ** is another version of this initialism, and the two terms are often used interchangeably depending on personal or political preference.

Despite the many different forms this initialism can take, the letters (and the

intention) are generally the same:
- For about 15 minutes in the '90s, there was GLBTO (O for "other").
- SGL in LGBTQ/SGL stands for "same gender loving," and tends to be more popular among people of color.
- More commonly, you will encounter
  - GLBTQI (I for "intersex")
  - GLBTQIA (A for "asexual")
  - LGBTQIAA (another A for "ally" or supporter)
  - GLBTTQIAA (another T for "transsexual" and/or "transgendered").
- A recent Canadian pride parade was marketed as LGBTTIQQ2SA to include the First Nation/ Native American concept of Two-Spirit.

You'll also sometimes see the use of asterisks or plus signs (GLBT* and LGBT+) as a shorthand to include myriad other groups, cohorts, and minorities that can make the terms impractical or confusing. The order of the letters is somewhat arbitrary, and it can morph into an unwieldy alphabet soup, but most everyone has a favorite. Individual identity can be loaded with feelings, and the different communities are not always united, but the whole point of this initialism is inclusion and identification, so focus on that, aim for respect, and don't be afraid to ask when you encounter a term or string of letters you're not familiar with.

Approximately 3.5 percent of the U.S. population identifies in the LGBT range.[3] That works out to approximately 9 million people; however, this number may be misleading. The figure most likely includes only people who are comfortable with their homosexuality (and are "out"), since people who are not out don't tend to publicly identify. "Out" means that you are open about your sexuality and tell people you are G, L, B, T, or Q.

It is hard to estimate exactly how many people are not straight and not out (or not out *yet*), but studies show that 1.8 percent of the population identifies as bisexual ("bi" for short); that's more than gay and lesbian combined, at 1.7 percent.[4] Ironically, the same study reported that bisexuals are less than half as likely to be out as gays and lesbians.

Bisexuality
In 1948, sexologist Alfred Kinsey created the Kinsey scale,[5] a questionnaire that served to rate a person's attraction and behavior with regard to sex along a continuum. The questionnaire asked people to rate on a scale of 0–6 whom they're attracted to physically, whom they're attracted to emotionally, and what they've done about it.

Kinsey found that most people have both heterosexual and homosexual thoughts and feelings, and that the majority of people engage in sex with people of both sexes at some point in their lives. This suggested that most people are some flavor of bisexual.

Most contemporary research agrees with this, and describes sexual identity as being very fluid — a continuum scale, rather than closed categories. This idea meshes with the general understanding that sexuality develops and can change in many ways over a person's lifetime. Most people do not stay in the exact same place on the scale for their entire life. Very few people think, feel, or do the same things sexually when they are fifteen as they do when they are twenty, forty, or sixty.

Most sex educators tend to reach the same general conclusions as Kinsey: Heterosexuality, bisexuality, and homosexuality make up a sexual identity continuum. Although they might gravitate to either the "gay" or "straight" end of this continuum, most people float somewhere in the middle, and many, many men and women experiment with same-sex sex at some point.

☛ *A special note about coming out:* "Coming out" is the process of accepting and being open about one's sexual orientation, particularly when one's orientation is not straight. This is part of being healthy, being true to yourself, and being "you" to the highest degree that you can be.

The opposite of this is called "closeted" (not out), as in "She is in the closet." The first stage of coming out is coming out to one's self; in other words, acknowledging your own sexual orientation. This may happen anytime between adolescence and adulthood. Exploring and deciding where we are on the spectrum between straight and gay is everyone's right and responsibility.

☛ *A special note about experimentation:* Experimentation is one way that some people help sort out where they are on that spectrum, trying sexual things with people of both sexes. As we decide whether we are chocolate or vanilla people, cake or pie people, Xbox or PlayStation people, and PC or Mac people, we come to decisions about which sides of certain fences we stand on by jumping those fences and trying different things.

Many straight people have done sexual things with someone of the same sex. Many gay people have done sexual things with someone of the opposite sex. These behaviors themselves do not make someone gay, or straight, or anything in between, but engaging in them is a way for us to figure out who we are.

Some people, however, are tempted to justify and explain repeated sexual acts with people of the same sex because they have a hard time being OK with it. If you have experimented with someone of the same sex more than three times in a relatively short amount of time (such as a summer, semester, or a week at band camp), you aren't "experimenting" anymore. Own it.

Cheesecake is the combination of rich yet light, creamy, and sweet cheese filling inside of a crunchy, buttery, graham-cracker crust. How many times do you think someone needs to "experiment" with cheesecake before they decide if they like it? Exactly.

It is not necessary to experiment or have sex with someone in order to identify as gay, bi, or straight. Trust your feelings, trust your gut, trust the thoughts that are going through your head when you masturbate, and when you think you are ready to have a go with another human, check out Part Two (page 35).

There are many theories about how sexuality develops, but one thing is for certain: Sexuality is no more a choice than ear shape, musical ability, or height.

Says who? Says the American Psychiatric Association, American Academy of Pediatrics, American Counseling Association, American Association of School Administrators, American Federation of Teachers, American School Health Association, Interfaith Alliance, National Association of School Psychologists, National Association of Social Workers, National Education Association, and World Health Organization.[6]

Like ear shape, musical ability, and height, sexuality is most likely a combination of biology and environment.[7] Biological influences on whether someone is straight, gay, both, neither, or somewhere in between include genes, prenatal hormones, and the structure of the brain. The environmental pieces can be more obvious in some ways and harder to pin down in others. Social and cultural stigmas, religion, politics, media, and laws get in the way of people being able to deal honestly with their own (and others') sexuality.

Things to consider if you think, wonder, worry, or believe you are some flavor of not-straight:
- What do you fantasize about while masturbating*?
- What pornography have you found yourself looking at*?
- Whom do you have romantic (not just sexual) feelings for?
- Are you bored with or pretending interest in the opposite sex?
- Do you feel like you are acting or playing the part of a straight person?
- Have you experimented more than three times with someone of the same sex?

*It is important to know that fantasies and porn themes are not necessarily indicators of orientation. Many people think about different sexual expressions than those they might act on in real life (see Chapter 21 for more). It's yet another opportunity to learn more about yourself.

Gay thoughts, feelings, and even acts do not make someone gay. Many gay adults have done sexual things with the opposite gender[8] — it didn't make them straight! *Repetitive* gay thoughts, feelings, and even acts may mean you are not straight. If this is the case, then it is a good idea to find someone to talk to, because the next stage is coming out to others.

☞ *Another special note about coming out:* Coming out can seem unfair in the sense that straight people do not have to sit down with friends and loved ones to let them know that they like the opposite sex and then answer those people's questions. But remember, it's not necessary for people who are not straight to tell anyone specific or gory details about their sex lives or practices. Although it is not unusual or unhealthy to keep aspects of our personal and sexual lives private, fighting against who you are, pretending to be someone you are not, or living a life in which you have to keep secrets or tell lies is exhausting, and cannot be done for long periods of time without causing problems.

For not-straight people, coming out is about being healthy, being true to yourself, and being the most "you" you can be. It allows you to act and speak freely about your day-to-day life without having to double-check or censor everything that comes out of your mouth.

The rules of coming out are very similar to that of a swimming pool.

First of all, have fun. Be proud and enjoy yourself, celebrate who you are, and surround yourself with people who want to do the same.

Wear sunscreen. Well, OK, not sunscreen, but do protect yourself. Safer not-straight sex can be different than what you have been taught, seen, tried, or even had to think about. Ask questions and educate yourself (see page 49) before you jump in and start swimming.

In fact, rather than jumping in, a good way to start the coming-out process is to **wade into the pool.** Opening up to one or two trusted friends or family members can help to slowly gather support as you build your confidence.

No running. Go slowly. Be prepared for some people to be shocked and possibly upset — particularly parents — and be gentle with them. Most parents experience a range of reactions when a child comes out. These reactions can range from "Does this mean I will never have grandchildren?" to worrying about your safety, to their own biases and prejudices from growing up in a different generation or culture. It is important to try not to take these reactions too personally.

Be patient. Give each person you come out to a few days to digest the new information, and invite them to ask questions (because they might not know how to, or may be afraid of upsetting or offending you).

Don't be too patient, though. After a few weeks, if your friends are still being weird about it, move on. Author and podcast host Dan Savage advocates that parents should get a year to freak out, be sad, etc., and then they need to get on board. Draw your lines in the sand and stick to them.

Keep an eye out for others. Do not be surprised to hear a few "me, toos" (a few "Polos" to your "Marco"), when you start coming out. It's hard to know who else is in the pool until you get your head underwater.

Safety first. Take care of yourself and surround yourself with resources and information, such as the It Gets Better Project (*itgetsbetter.org*) or your school's Gay-Straight Alliance (GSA). Note to straight girls: They are called "Gay-Straight Alliances." If you are cool with the gays — have friends or family members who are gay — join up and show some support.

Don't splash those who are not in the pool. It is never cool to out someone else.

Coming out helps build self esteem and a capacity for intimacy. But it can be very stressful, sometimes harming self-esteem in the process. Dealing with gay thoughts and feelings (let alone coming out) is a difficult process, and can result in feelings of isolation and societal stigmas stemming from fear, bigotry, and hatred.

Gay kids account for 30 percent of all teen suicides[9] and 30 percent of gays and lesbians report that they have attempted suicide at some point in their life.[10] Most gay people prior to the 1970s were closeted because of fear of being mistreated or victimized; being gay was even considered a mental illness until the mid-1970s.[11]

Today, it is much safer for someone to come out and be out, although many gay people still have to struggle with negative stereotypes, media misinformation, and fear — all of which is called "homophobia."

☛ *A special note about homophobia:* Homophobia is fear, hatred, and/or discrimination against gay people. Hatred of gay people comes from fear. That fear comes from ignorance, and/or from people's reactions to their own gay thoughts and feelings.

Homophobia is a social disease, like racism, sexism, or other kinds of bigotry. It is unfair, harmful, and too often becomes violent. This kind of violence is called "gay bashing," and is considered a hate crime.[12] It's the same as when someone is victimized because of the color of their skin or their religious beliefs.

There are some terms that are considered homophobic: "fag" (or "faggot"), "dyke," and "queer." Like "nigger" and other racist slurs, these words are designed to insult and humiliate people based on qualities they cannot control or change. It is never cool to shame, tease, be hateful to, or treat someone differently for something they have no control over.

Also, as with "nigger" and other racist slurs, some minority groups have attempted to reclaim the negative terms, using them amongst and in reference to themselves as a way to lessen the impact and pain those words are associated with. It is only acceptable to use those taken-back terms if you are "in the club," like black guys calling one another "nigga," or gay girls calling each other "dyke." If you are not in a particular club (or close enough to someone who is invited to the picnic), using these terms is extremely insensitive and disrespectful, and should be avoided.

Like "retarded," using "gay" as an insult (as in: "That shirt is so gay") should be considered a very big no-no. People who use these offensive terms as insults should probably be avoided, as well.

Although the vast majority of educated therapists and researchers state that sexual orientation is unchangeable, there are still people who believe the opposite — that conversion (also called reparative therapy) is possible and effective. These people believe that people can choose their sexuality (people can't). Some try to use prayer, counseling, and even drugs to try to "cure" gay people. These techniques are never aimed at straight people.

Therapy can be helpful for people who are troubled by their sexuality, or are struggling emotionally or socially, but according to the American Psychiatric Association, there is no evidence that any treatment can change a homosexual person's feelings for others of the same sex. There is no published scientific evidence supporting the efficacy of reparative therapy as a treatment to change anyone's sexual orientation.[13]

Changing a person's sexual orientation would not simply be about changing behavior. It would involve altering someone's emotional, romantic, and sexual feelings, as well as re-creating one's entire self-concept and social identity. People can change their behavior, but not their internal experience. You can't turn or unturn gay. Gay thoughts, feelings, and even actions do not make you gay, but they can help you figure out who and what you are.

☛ *Another note about coming out:* Coming out as trans looks different than coming out as gay. Coming out as gay is the process of accepting and being open about one's sexual orientation. This is part of being healthy, being true to yourself, and being the most "you" that you can be. For trans people, being healthy, being true to themselves, and being the most "they" that they can be means living as or transitioning to their authentic gender. This may or may not include having others know you are trans.[14]

Coming out is about being healthy and true to yourself. Coming out as gay is about telling. Coming out as trans is often more about showing. This is often done through dress and modifying one's appearance (cross-dressing).

Transsexuals can also seek medical interventions, such as hormones and surgery, to make their bodies as congruent as possible with their gender. The process of changing from one gender to another is called **sex reassignment** or **gender reassignment.**

People who are attracted to women prior to transition generally continue to be attracted to women after transition, and people who are attracted to men prior to transition generally continue to be attracted to men after transition. That means, for example, that a biological male who is attracted to females will still be attracted to females after making the transition, and may regard herself as a lesbian (though the sexuality of a transsexual can be as fluid as anyone else's).

☛ *OK, one more note about coming out:* Coming and being "out" is a process that is continual. Although not being out for extended periods of time can cause problems, it is important to remember to keep context in mind. For people who live in a place, culture, or family in which an alternative sexuality or identity is unwelcome, it may be smarter or safer to wait to come out until circumstances change. As an adult, you will have more opportunity and ability to create your safe spaces than you do as an adolescent.

Gender Expression and the Spectrum
Gender expression refers to one's dress, demeanor, and deeds, the relationship

of those things to one's sexual and gender identity, and how they are interpreted by others.

Androgynous is an example of an identity within the spectrum of gender expression. An androgynous person
  • does not fit cleanly into typical masculine and feminine roles, and/or
  • is able to draw from both traditionally masculine and feminine qualities.

Your gender expression is connected to, but not dependent on, your sexual orientation.

People generally experience sex, gender, orientation, and expression as different things. While aspects of biological sex are the same across different cultures, aspects of sexuality, such as gender and expression, may not be.

Self-identity and sexual orientation both form slowly over time and in the context of life experiences. Sexuality is very fluid, and how a person identifies today is not necessarily how they did in the past or will in the future. No one should feel pressured to label themselves until they are ready, but it is important to find someone to talk to about any troubling thoughts and feelings. Talking to a trusted friend, adult, doctor, or teacher is especially important if you have felt targeted, threatened, harmed, or abused because of your identity or orientation.

PART TWO
RELATIONSHIPS AND CHOICES

CHAPTER 5
Dating and Communicating

When it comes to relationships, hardly anyone is taught how to get started — to find the right person and then ask them out.

Some of the best ways to find a person you might want to date include
- going to a place where there are other people doing something you enjoy — the concert of a favorite band, a friend's soccer game, a class about something that interests you;
- doing interesting things that others would want to hear or talk about, such as reading a popular book at lunch, or joining a group or team;
- doing research to familiarize yourself with things that a person you like is interested in.

Once you've found the person you want to date, it's OK to ask them out. Even though society sometimes sends messages that girls are supposed to just sit around waiting for someone to ask them first, it is totally OK (and, in fact, very cool) to ask. You can do this via text message, though you score points for bravery, class, vulnerability, and romance if you can cowgirl up and do it in person.

Making small talk can help. Small talk is made up of a very simple three-step formula:
1. **Statement.** This is where you make a comment, such as:
    "Hey, you sit behind me in math class, yeah?"
    "Man, it smells so good out here today!"
    "Cool party."

2. **Disclosure.** This is where you reveal something personal about yourself, such as:
    "I can't wait to graduate and never do algebra again!"
    "Fall is my favorite season — the smells, the colors, the food ... "
    "This song sucks, though."

3. **Connection.** This is where you ask them a (not "yes" or "no") question, such as:
    "Are you into math? How did you do on that last test?"

"If there could only be one season, which one would you choose?"
"How do you know [*insert name of party host*]?"

Eventually, you'll want to move beyond small talk to a very specific invitation. "I'm thinking about going to see [*insert name of band, art show, or a movie that is not a total chick-flick*] on Saturday afternoon. Would you like to come with me?" is better than, "Do you want to go out sometime?"

How to let someone know you are interested

It never hurts to get to know people as friends first — it can make dating a lot less stressful and a lot more interesting. Other tips for showing interest:

- Smile.
- Say "hello."
- Speak to them like they're a relative you actually like.
- Make eye contact. Hold their gaze for one second longer than is comfortable for you, then look away.
- The second time you make eye contact, smile again.
- Ask open-ended questions. That means questions the other person can't answer with just a simple "yes" or "no."
- Keep the conversation flowing. If they are interested, they will help you do this.
- Learn to spend time alone. It's hard to find someone who wants to spend time with you if you can't do it yourself.
- Learn to pay attention to the kind of people you are interested in, how they make you feel, and how they treat you. You are one-half of all the relationships you are in. Being aware of negative patterns is important in helping to make sure you are choosing people who will make you happy.

☛ *A special note about flirting:* Flirting is fun and sexy, and it boosts both people's egos. On the other hand, sexual harassment is not fun, not sexy, and only boosts one person's ego. The line between the two can be crossed when
- it is one-sided;
- it focuses on the other person's body rather than the other person;
- there is a difference in power (boss/employee, coach/athlete, senior/ freshman, etc.);
- it is done in the workplace;
- one person becomes embarrassed, creeped out, insulted, or scared;
- you are doing or saying something you would not do in front of other people;
- you are doing or saying something that would upset you if it were done or said to you (or someone you care about).

How to know when someone is interested in return
Good signs from a boy:
- a smile that shows teeth
- touching of any kind
- an audible laugh
- a look back after you pass each other

Good signs from another girl:
- a smile that shows teeth
- touching of any kind
- an audible laugh
- primping in general, but specifically anything involving her lips or hair
- an introduction to her friends

☛ *A special note about dating:* Your first date should be fun, light, and public. Here are some good rules of thumb:
- To avoid uncomfortable first-date situations, try meeting at your date destination.
- If you are meeting there, be five minutes early. Arriving early helps you get comfortable and relaxed, and lowers your date's stress if that person can walk in and find you easily.
- Have plenty of cash to cover the bill.
- Be willing (and prepared) to talk about yourself and ask the other person questions about himself or herself. Politics, money, religion, and exes are generally off-limits topics.
- Be honest, be polite, be yourself, and expect nothing more at the end of the date than a kiss on the cheek.

☛ *A special note about online dating:* Online dating is creative, commonplace, exciting, and exhausting. In this day and age, you are officially more likely to ask/be asked out via a screen than in real life.

To be clear, when online (just like in real life), there is a difference between hooking up (getting together for the purpose of sex) and dating. Many hook-up apps try to disguise themselves as dating apps, and many people (particularly males) use dating sites as hook-up sites. Be aware of this when using dating apps and sites. Hook-up apps are designed for adults and can be dangerous for teens.

Online dating is legit, and many people are meeting, creating great relationships, and even getting married through online dating, though it more often results in a couple of dates and a fadeaway. Still, there is something magical about spending time becoming clear about what you want and don't want in a partner, and then putting that out there for like-minded people to respond.

However, online dating should really be called online meeting. It's a great way to make a connection, but not for actively connecting. It's great for speed and volume, but not always substance or actually getting to know another person. Many people have become trained to automatically choose or reject while screening potential relationship prospects, as though we are scrolling through an Amazon wishlist. Relationships are more than swiping right or hitting the "like" button.

Online dating can put you in contact with interesting people quite easily, but it's important to remember that the work of actual emotional and physical intimacy is harder, and involves things like being vulnerable (as opposed to posting a staged selfie), wanting to be with a specific someone (not amassing an endless queue of online profiles), transparency and truly being seen (not as a curated profile or an emoji), cuddling (not an up vote), even being naked with someone (as opposed to a sultry photo).

The good news is that online dating can help you build muscles of banter and conversation that can make face-to-face discussions in real life easier as well. Just remember that online dating is meant to create opportunities for real-life intimacy. If real relationships were as easy as the ones online, everyone would be in one.

Other dating tips:
- Dating is expensive; it costs money, time, and emotions. If you're not able or willing to expend these things, find a different way to connect.
- If you're not going to call or text, don't say you will.
- If you say you will, do it — within two days.
- If anything physical happens that couldn't be shown on The Disney Channel, call the next day.
- Make sure there's been at least one Saturday-night date by date number three.

Letting someone know you're not interested
Even though roles can be fluid in our culture, we have collectively decided that it is typically the boy's job to ask for a date, and the girl's job to say yes or no. Both jobs are equally difficult, and if the other person is not making the situation stressful, neither should you. No one likes to be rejected.

If you're not interested, or no longer interested, be nice about it.

Also be clear about it. As a therapist and sex educator who has worked with boys for the past several years (and being one myself), I know how difficult it is for most guys when the person they're interested in is not clear. It feels less civilized but is actually much more humane to offer a clear "no," if that is what the answer is. Vague and noncommittal answers are nobody's friend. In general, guys would rather have clarity than a cushioned ego, a definitive answer rather than the prolonged ache and confusion of wondering and hoping. In extremely rare cases, turning down a guy might lead to aggression – those guys are out there – but the vast majority will not respond to rejection with violence.

If you ever do feel unsafe, seek help from a parent, a teacher, a counselor, or some other trusted adult (see page 43).

How do you let someone of the same sex know that you are no longer interested? The same way you would tell someone who is of the opposite sex. This should never include insults, threats, or violence of any kind.

I work very hard in my practice to encourage and teach teens to focus on the friendship and the intimacy as much as the foxy and the sexy. In this light, asking out someone you are already friends with is a sign of maturity.

If you must turn a friend down, do it quickly, humanely, and in service to the kind of relationship you want to have afterward. If you can take the compliment, find the fun and humor in it (and maybe even offer to step up into the wing-woman role afterward), it doesn't necessarily need to be weird.

Other tips
Powerful women speak their minds and let the other person do the same. They are honest, nonviolent, and accept responsibility for their choices, instead of trying to place blame on the other person. Breaking up with someone is different from asking someone out (see above regarding: bravery and class). If you have seen someone in their underwear, then you must break up in person. Breaking up with someone via text is both cowardly and lame. Choose not to be That Girl.

Ghosting (deciding you aren't interested anymore and disappearing without an explanation or closure) is not cool. Don't be her, either.

The ability to remain friends with exes, and friends who were "almost," is typically a sign of a good person (as opposed to a girl who can't be friends with any of her exes or almosts). People notice that stuff.

When you must break up with someone, do it quickly, not publicly, and nowhere near the date of the other person's birthday or a major holiday.

How to know if a relationship is good for you

There are many things that factor into a relationship, but this list is a good start for figuring out the strength of a relationship. Are the following qualities part of your current relationship?

- respect
- honesty
- trust
- fairness
- talking/listening
- boundaries
- needs
- support
- love
- sex

In healthy relationships, there are sometimes unhealthy behaviors that can be improved. Partners can talk about them and work on them. Sometimes relationships are unhealthy, and sometimes even healthy relationships have unhealthy parts that cannot be fixed. The goal is to know which of these relationships you are in.

Good partners:

- **Do not try to control you.** Preventing you from having friends, interfering with your choices, or giving you orders are signs that your partner is controlling. You do not have to put up with this.
- **Do not emotionally abuse you.** Some people need to tear you down to make themselves feel better (or at least make you afraid to leave them because they seem like the only one who would ever put up with the mess that is you). This is called emotional abuse, and you don't have to put up with this, either.
- **Do not disrespect you.** Good partners are not afraid of equality. A partner who is condescending, insulting you or putting you down about your thoughts, feelings, brain, body, or heart is not a good partner. A partner who is constantly explaining how he or she is more powerful/smart/interesting/whatever than you is only trying to convince you that you are less than.
- **Do not invade your privacy.** In a healthy relationship, there is no need to hide big things from your partner. That being said, privacy is a thing, and your partners don't need to have your passwords, access to your feeds, or the right to snoop through your bags, journals, or tech. Doing so without reason or consent is creepy and should not be tolerated.
- **Do not use trust as a weapon.** Having someone distrust you when you've done something untrustworthy is legitimate. You know yourself; you look at yourself in the mirror before you go to sleep at night. If you legitimately have

done nothing to earn someone's suspicion, then don't put up with it. Do not start a game of trying to earn trust from someone who mistrusts you for no reason. That is a trap.

- **Do not make you feel too far down their list.** A relationship is a part of life, not life itself. Just as no partner should ever be a higher priority on your list than you are, your partner should be focused on his or her own goals, self-worth, and individuality. You should not expect to be number one on anyone's list but your own. Number two is a great position to shoot for, but there are times when things like school, jobs, physical health, parents, or (eventually) kids may need to take a higher slot on our own lists. These things shift and morph as time passes and intimacy grows. But if you find that you are consistently lower down on your partner's list than you want to be, talk about it. Being a priority is different than being a primary focus or an afterthought.
- **Do not make you do all the work.** A relationship is about teamwork. Relationships can become difficult as energy levels, personal feelings, and emotions fluctuate. The ups and downs of the rest of our lives invade our relationships. We need to be prepared for this to happen, ride the waves, and do our legit best for our partners. And we should expect them to do this, too.
- **Do not avoid conflict.** No one particularly likes conflict, but problems can't be resolved until they are faced. Avoidance of difficult topics and situations stops a relationship from progressing and potentially makes the problems worse.
- **Do not cheat on you.** There are plenty of examples of monogamy not being the natural, default state for humans. Some people may not be wired to spend long periods of time with one person. But if you are clear about your commitment and expectations, then a good partner is going to do her or his best to hold to that commitment, and take responsibility and repair it if she or he doesn't.

There are a ton of messages in popular media that anytime anyone crosses over the line of monogamy, the relationship is ruined and must end. In reality, people screw up, and this may happen to you (or your partner), but if the one who screwed up can take responsibility, apologize, and repair the relationship, it can ultimately make the relationship even stronger. Monogamy does not have to be the default, but if you or your sexual partner are also partnering sexually or romantically with others, there should be conversation, clarity, and consent.

☛ *A special note about players:* A player is a person who is good at making people think he or she is into them and/or dates several people at once without letting them know about it. "Player" is another word for cheater or manipulator. This is not a person who dates many people in an open or consensual way. It's someone who hurts people because that person either doesn't know or doesn't care about what a real relationship is.

All of us are 50 percent of the relationships we are in. Making sure we are aware of our negative patterns and habits is important to help ensure we are treating people well and choosing people who make us happy.

Some people think they can change players — tame them and make them behave properly. I do not think players can be tamed by their partners. (FYI, Getting into any relationship in which you feel the need to alter a significant aspect of the other person's personality is not generally going to end well.)

I think players need to tame themselves. And this can happen — it takes time, maturity (BTW, not the same thing), and experiences, such as having people call them on their game playing, refuse to put up with their self-centered behavior, or make them suffer the consequences of a negative reputation.

Lastly, I would encourage anyone out there screening for players to check yourself as well. Players are attracted to (in fact, encouraged by) people who are willing to be pawns and fall for their tricks. Have conversations with your friends and watch each other's backs.

It is important to pay attention to the people you are interested in and drawn to; to how those people make you feel and how they treat you.

Do you always choose people who
- make you feel bad about yourself?
- cheat?
- don't trust you?
- are unobtainable?
- ask you to do things you don't want to do?
- hate your parents?
- need to be fixed?

Being able to think about your relationships objectively and being aware of your patterns (healthy and otherwise) are necessary skills for dating. The good news is, once you identify a pattern, you have the power to change it.

Other things to keep your eye on: How does he or she treat other women out in the world? You can tell a lot about a person by watching how well they play with others. Are they rude to the barista? Do they talk smack about their exes? Make fun of the fat girl across the room? Make that old lady open the door by herself? These are clues to character.

☛ *A special note about dating violence:* Dating violence (also called intimate violence) is abusive, aggressive, and controlling behavior in a relationship, either straight or gay. People who are not in a romantic or a dating relationship can do intimate violence to each other as well.

There are different types of intimate violence, including verbal, physical, sexual, and/or digital abuse.

Verbal (or emotional) abuse includes things like threats, insults, intimidation, isolation, and stalking.

Physical abuse includes things like shoving, hitting, choking, or anything that leaves bruises.

Sexual abuse includes anything that takes away your ability to control how, where, or when you engage in sexual contact. It includes rape, unwanted touch, messing with your access to birth control, or pressuring you to have sex.

Digital abuse includes using tech or the Internet to harass someone else. Things like invading privacy, bullying, threatening, unwanted images or messages, and cyberstalking fall into this category.

Anyone can be a victim of dating violence. Boys and girls are (almost) equally likely to be both victims and perpetrators of dating violence[1], but boys and girls tend to abuse their partners in different ways.

A study funded by the CDC found that 41 percent of girls ages 14–20 reported being a victim of dating violence and that 35 percent reported engaging in some form of dating violence toward their partner. For boys, 37 percent said they had been on the receiving end, while 29 percent reported being the perpetrator. Girls are more likely to yell, threaten to hurt themselves as a manipulation, or slap their partners. Boys are more likely to punch their partner or force them into unwanted sexual activity.[2]

Abusive people have problems, try to make everyone else around them as miserable as they are, and do not tend to stop without some sort of consequence, classes, or counseling.

Leave. Block. Tell.

If you wouldn't stand by and let them physically injure a puppy, then you sure as hell shouldn't allow them to do it to you.

If you have a partner who lays hands on you (not in a good way):
- Do not make excuses for their behavior. This communicates that such behavior is OK, and it begins to lower your tolerance for this nonsense.
- Do not think it is your fault.
- Leave, block, unfriend, unfollow, etc.
- Tell someone, so you can get the support you need to stop being harmed any further and to prevent someone else from getting hurt.

Important things to know about dating violence:
- Dating violence can be especially confusing, because it involves someone you care about and who supposedly cares about you.
- One out of three teens is a victim of dating violence.
- Dating violence rarely stops on its own.
- Dating violence usually gets worse over time.
- Hitting a boyfriend or a girlfriend is a crime. It is against the law.
- The best thing you can do is to be watchful for signs of abuse, both against yourself and others, and say something if and when you see it.

Signs of an abusive relationship include a partner who
- checks your devices, social media accounts, or email without permission;
- uses actions to show anger (rather than words);
- shows jealousy (with anger);
- shows insecurity (with anger);
- is constantly putting you down;
- isolates you from family or friends;
- makes false accusations;
- physically hurts you (in any way);
- tells you what to do; and/or
- pressures or forces you to have sex.

Report concerns about dating violence to
- your parents
- a teacher or school administrator
- the National Teen Dating Abuse Helpline: 866-331-9474 (or text "loveis" to 22522)
- your local police

Communication

The first rule of communication: If you can't talk about it, you shouldn't be doing it. You and your intimate partner should be able to communicate about

- the names of body parts
- the names of sexual acts
- your body
- his or her body
- your past sexual behaviors
- definitions of things like "sex" and "virginity"
- what you want
- what you don't want
- safer sex methods

Tips for Good Communication

A large chunk of communication has to do with what comes out of your mouth. Try using "I" statements — statements that begin with "I think," "I feel," and "I want." They can help you make yourself clear without putting others on the defensive (as can happen when you start out by saying "You ... ").

Open-ended questions encourage people to talk and continue the conversation ("What are you upset about?" or "What do you think of ... ?"), instead of conversation stoppers ("Are you still mad?" "Do you wanna ... ?").

Another big chunk of communication has to do with what goes into your ears. Listening to others makes them more likely to listen in return. People have a hard time knowing you're listening unless you show them. Listen between the words and try to figure out what the other person thinks and feels. When you think you have it figured out, check it out by asking clarifying questions (which means clearing up any confusing parts or words that they have just said: "Do you mean ... ?") and paraphrasing (which means restating what they just said in a different way to show them that you understand: "It sounds like you're saying ... ").

Show your partner that you respect them enough to ask about their sexual needs and desires. If you are not accustomed to communicating with your partner about sex and sexual activity, the first few times may feel awkward, but with practice, it gets a little better each time as you and your partner become more secure in yourselves and your relationship. The more times that you have these conversations, the more comfortable you will both become.

This will never go perfectly.

Ideally, sexual behavior between two people should be viewed as teamwork. You are in this together, and if it is more difficult to have a conversation with your partner about sex than it is to actually *have* sex, that's a good indication that you should probably wait a bit longer.

If you can't talk about it, you shouldn't be doing it.

☛ *A special note about technology:* Communication is the most important factor in a relationship. A lot of communication occurs via technology, but relationships that occur only between screens are not actual relationships.

Cues such as emotional expression, body language, and intuition are very important in healthy relationships — especially as a relationship grows closer to becoming sexual. You cannot read a facial gesture, fall into that sweet spot of hesitation right before a kiss, or tell if it's OK to put your hand on someone's butt via text message, Skype, or social networking.

Balance your screen relationships with actual, real-time human contact. And do not say or do anything via a screen that you would not say or do if the person was standing in front of you. (This includes randomly sending someone pictures of your breasts.)

P.S. Stop doing that.

CHAPTER 6
Sexual Arousal

Unlike other animals, humans do not have a mating season, although sexual arousal and response is a cycle in both men and women. The human arousal cycle has four basic parts: excitement, plateau, orgasm, and resolution.[1]

Excitement (or arousal) is the horny part, when you are interested in sex, are feeling attracted to someone, or are actively turned on. The body responds to this with increased temperature and blood flow to the genitals, creating erections in men and moisture for women.

During male arousal, blood flows into the spongy erectile tissue inside the penis, causing it to elongate and become erect (get hard). Female arousal starts with the swelling of the areas around the vagina, erection of the clitoris and nipples, and secretion of lubricating fluids in the vagina (getting wet). Stimulation of the genitals through friction causes the nervous system to fire up sensory receptors in the penis, vaginal walls, anus, and clitoris. The sperm leave the testicles and join secretions of other glands to form semen.

Plateau is the highest point of sexual excitement. That's when you're actively engaged in sexual activity.

Orgasm is the peak of the plateau stage and the point at which sexual tension is released, creating waves of pleasurable sensations as well as muscular contractions of the penis (male) or vagina (female) and anus (both), which eventually end in intense feelings called an orgasm. This is often accompanied by ejaculation. Ejaculation is also called "coming," as well as many other things.

It is important to note that orgasm and ejaculation are not the same thing. Ejaculation is the discharge of fluids; orgasm is the big, good feeling.

Both men and women orgasm. Although the experiences are similar, there are differences between the male and the female orgasm. Men reach orgasm most typically through the rubbing of the head of their penis (the glans), but can also reach orgasm through stimulation of their prostate. Some women reach orgasm through vaginal penetration (with fingers, penises, or penis-shaped tools and toys such as vibrators or dildos, in order to stimulate the G-spot), but almost 80 percent of women also need clitoral stimulation to achieve orgasm.[2] Many women masturbate by only rubbing their clitoris.

Orgasms from stimulation of the glans or clitoris tend to focus inward (picture the Death Star's laser at the beginning of *Star Wars*). Orgasms through stimulating the G-spot or prostate tend to focus outward (think of the Death Star blowing up at the end of *Star Wars*).

Both men and women ejaculate. Some women emit fluid from their urethra during orgasm; this is called female ejaculation. There is a female counterpart to the male prostate, technically known as Skene's glands, embedded in the wall of the urethra. Just like the male prostate, the ducts from these glands create secretions in women. This fluid's primary purpose is the lubrication of the vagina. It is similar to semen (without sperm), and some women can actually expel (or ejaculate) this liquid.

Men ejaculate semen (also called "come" or "cum"), the combination of sperm and other liquids gathered along the way. The average guy ejaculates about a teaspoon of fluids, and each teaspoon contains approximately 600 million spermatozoa.[3] The reason there are so many of them is because sperm are very sensitive; they are easily damaged and affected by heat, time, and the acidity of both the urethra and the vagina. In the end, fewer than 1,000 sperm make it to the egg; typically, just one gets in.

Resolution is the body returning to its normal, unexcited state. This tends to happen fairly quickly after orgasm as blood flow returns to normal and genital excitement subsides. During this stage, genitals can become extremely sensitive, ticklish, or even painful to the touch. This sensation is part of resolution and will pass rather quickly. The **refractory period** is the time between when someone has an orgasm and when they can have another one. Women tend to be able to do this much faster than men.

CHAPTER 7
Sexual Activity

People's sexual likes, dislikes, needs, and wants are as different as our personalities. What someone really likes, someone else may not. What one person is excited about may be scary to another.

Our choices are greatly influenced by myths and misinformation that we get from television, music, movies, and the Internet. These things might have some people believing that men need to be aggressive and women are supposed to be passive, or that men are supposed to have 10-inch penises, and women should enjoy it when they do. (BTW, in both cases, most do not.)

We are taught to believe that people scream and moan during sex, and do it in places such as bathtubs. We are taught that everyone knows what they are doing, that they do it for forty-five minutes, and that they orgasm every time they have sex and always at the same time as their partner. (Again, BTW: not.)

Orgasm does not need to be the be-all-and-end-all, whole point of sex. Orgasm does not mean that everything went right and everyone got what they wanted. Not having an orgasm does not mean that something went wrong. There are plenty of things to do and plenty of fun to be had without that big finish.

This usually makes less sense to boys than it does to girls, because it sounds like playing football without any touchdowns, but keep in mind that your largest sexual organ is your skin, and your most important sexual organ is your brain.

Sex is an urge human animals have — not a lot different than eating or sleeping.[1] There are different kinds of sexual intercourse, and a whole load of different things that are part of sexual activity. This is because the drive is not voluntary, but the behavior is. It's like eating: We all need to eat for survival, but some people eat veggies and brown rice, and some eat fast food five times a week.

There are no universal positions or patterns that work for everyone. There is nothing wrong with making yourself and/or someone else feel good as long as
- you and your partner are comfortable with what you are doing,
- you are doing it safely,
- you are doing it legally,
- you are aware of the consequences,
- no one (including yourself) is getting hurt.

Masturbation

Masturbation, aka "manual sex" or "jilling off" (or "jacking off" for guys), is sexual stimulation of one's own genitals to achieve sexual arousal, usually to the point of orgasm. This stimulation can also be performed by other people, by objects, or by other types of bodily contact.

The clitoris is the part that most women pay attention to during masturbation. The tiny head of the clitoris is similar to a penis (and also called the glans). Even though the glans of a clitoris is much, much smaller than the glans of a penis, it can contain many more nerve receptors.

Most girls masturbate by rubbing their clitoris with a finger. Some girls prefer lubrication; others prefer a dry hand. Some girls hump blankets or pillows or use devices that cause vibration such as a vibrator or showerhead. Some girls enjoy penetrating themselves with a finger or dildo. Girls can masturbate while lying in bed, sitting in a chair, or lying in the tub (strive to not to leave the water running for long periods of time; the earth is in terrible enough shape as it is without wasting water).

Masturbation should obviously be done in private. The only generally accepted places to masturbate are in your bedroom or in the bathroom. Avoid other people's bedrooms and your living room. Jilling off in public places, such as at school, in your car, or anywhere near a webcam is not a good thing.

☛ *A special note about safer safe sex:* By definition, masturbation is considered "safe" sex, as it is nearly impossible to become pregnant or get an STI while doing so. That said, it is important to make sure you are being nice to your body while masturbating so you don't hurt yourself.
- Beware of anything that might cut, burn, or otherwise injure your genitals.
- Anything involving more electricity than a couple of AA batteries should be suspect, as should anything that causes suction or could break.
- Anything that you think of placing inside your vagina should come out.
- Avoid inserting anything breakable and any kind of food, and screen lubricants for ingredients that can irritate the inside of your vagina (see page 62).
- Watch your fingernails, both in terms of the scraping factor, but also in terms of the bacteria that our hands naturally collect throughout the day, which can make vaginas very uncomfortable.

Some people do not masturbate, although most do — it's estimated that approximately 95 percent of men and almost 90 percent of women masturbate.[2] Masturbation often begins in adolescence and continues through adulthood. Although most people do it at some point in their lives, masturbation is not a common topic of conversation for most people.

The word itself is hundreds of years old and Latin in origin: manstuprare — a combination of two Latin words, *manus* (hand) and *stuprare* (defile).[3] So the word means, basically, to pollute yourself with your hand. This created a built-in association with shame, which has carried into modern times. Masturbation is still associated with guilt and anxiety, mostly because people believe that it is somehow harmful, and also because of centuries of religious teaching that it is sinful.

Many people have received negative messages about masturbation from their parents, or know someone who was "caught" masturbating. Has anyone ever heard of someone being "caught" brushing their teeth?

Masturbation is often the topic of insults, gross-out jokes, and teen comedy movies, which contribute to the guilt and confusion for some people.

Masturbation does not make you
  • blind
  • gay
  • deaf
  • crazy
  • grow hair on your hands
  • run out of sperm
  • stupid
  • die — or anyone around you die
  • sick
  • a loser

Masturbation is a natural and harmless expression of sexuality in both men and women, and a perfectly good way to experience sexual pleasure without the risks of pregnancy or disease. It also
  • releases sexual tension;
  • reduces stress and can help you sleep;[4]
  • helps you become more comfortable with your own body, sexuality, and fantasy life, making you better prepared for sexual activity with a partner later;
  • makes for a fun alternative to intercourse with a partner, reducing your chance of pregnancy and disease.

Sexual Fantasies
Sexual fantasies are the things we think about when thinking about sex, touching ourselves, or engaging in sex with others. They can be fun, sexy, and powerful, and

a great accompaniment to both masturbation and sexual activity with other people. They can even be an *alternative* to sexual activity with someone else, when you just talk about things you'd like to do, but wait until later to do them.

They can be about what we'd really like in real life, and they can be far from anything we'd ever actually want in real life. This is why they are called fantasy.

In fantasy, we can play with location, desire, orientations. Fantasies can involve people we know, celebrities or acquaintances we'd like to know better, or individuals we've made up in our heads. Everyone has sexual fantasies; they are perfectly safe and natural, and they can be a great way for us to get to know ourselves better and help us communicate our wants and dislikes to others.

That said, if you find yourself fantasizing about things that are disturbing to you, or if you find yourself thinking about things that would be unethical or illegal in real life, such as rape, or sex with animals or children, it is OK to talk to a counselor or a therapist to help sort out what is going on.

☛ *A special note about wet dreams:* Many people experience nocturnal orgasms, more commonly known as "wet dreams." For guys, a wet dream is when a buildup of sperm is spontaneously ejaculated while he's sleeping, but orgasming while you are asleep can happen to girls, too. This sometimes happens while we are dreaming about sex, though not always.

Nocturnal orgasms may wake you up (or not), and may leave evidence in the form of a discharge (or not). Not everyone has wet dreams, and those who do have fewer and fewer as they begin masturbating, become sexually active, and grow older.

Sex Toys
Sex toys are devices designed for penetration of the vagina or anus, and are used by people of all genders and orientations for masturbation (and sometimes during sex with a partner).

There are lots of different kinds of toys, and they can range in type, size, and shape from big to small, and from silly-looking to a bit scary. The most common types are vibrators and dildos.

Vibrators are exactly what they sound like: plastic cylindrical wands that contain batteries and can be switched on to buzz pleasurably.

Dildos are very similar to vibrators in shape, but lack the vibrating aspect. They can be made from wood, glass, metal, plastic, or rubber, and are often shaped to look like an actual penis.

Women can rub the vibrator on their clitoris or insert it into their vagina. Men can massage their penis, perineum, or anus, and some people of both sexes enjoy inserting vibrators into their bums. There are dildos specifically designed for anuses, often referred to as butt plugs, which have a flared base at the end so there is no way that the entire thing could accidentally get inserted or lost in (and later embarrassingly removed by emergency room staff from) someone's butt.

Once you believe yourself to be old enough to become sexually active with something besides your own hand (see page 67), sex toys such as vibrators and dildos can be a nice way to safely explore sexual feelings, help you develop a relationship with your own body, and provide a safe way to be sexual without involving another person.

Sex toys are generally difficult for minors to purchase, but through the Internet or perhaps a sorta awkward conversation with your parent/s or a trusted adult friend, all things are possible. Two reputable stores that not only sell toys, but also provide a staff of cool, approachable folks who can answer questions in a nonjudgmental way are *smittenkittenonline.com* and *babeland.com*.

Rules: In general, sex toys should
- not be shared;
- be covered by a barrier such as a condom and/or cleaned properly in between uses — especially anything used near your anus;
- come with cleaning instructions, although antibacterial soap and warm water will take care of most toys;
- not smell super plasticky or like a brand-new car;
- be disposed of after any cracks, rusting, or other irregularities are found;
- be used with lube when possible. Lube is your friend (see page 62);
- be stored in a clean, cool, dry place without their batteries;
- not be left out for company, roommates, or family members to find, because, eww.

☞ *A special note about phthalates:* Phthalates (pronounced "thay-lates") are chemicals that make plastics bendable. They are present in thousands of products, including raincoats, garden hoses, inflatable pool toys, scented candles, camping gear, cosmetics, cleaning products, and even medical supplies and children's toys. The human health effects of phthalates are not yet fully known, but they are being studied by several agencies, including the Food and Drug Administration, the National Institute of Environmental Health Sciences, and the National Toxicology

Program's Center for the Evaluation of Risks to Human Reproduction.[4]

Some medical professionals believe that exposure to phthalates can be damaging to human reproductive systems, among other things. Phthalates can be shed by plastic products as they deteriorate over time, so exposure to phthalates can happen quite easily when using plastic products — especially ones that have access to the insides of our bodies, such as plastic water containers and, yes, sex toys.

Until more studies are done, it's probably a good practice to avoid jelly or "bendy" sex toys that do not list their ingredients. Toys that are phthalate-free will say so on their packaging, although there is also a "sniff test": Any toy or product that contains phthalates will emit a plasticky smell, like as that of a shower curtain or a new rubber Halloween mask. The smellier it is, the more likely it is to contain phthalates.

Bottom line: There is nothing wrong with you if you masturbate. In fact, the only times masturbation can be harmful is when it becomes compulsive; when it takes up so much of your thoughts, time, and energy that it starts to cause problems in other areas of your life.

This is also an argument against pornography, as the two things are unfortunately linked on a fairly regular basis. Compulsive masturbation and/or use of pornography (like all other compulsive behaviors) is a sign of an emotional problem that needs to be addressed with the help of a counselor or therapist. Pay attention to the notes about porn throughout this book, and if you do choose to look at porn, make sure you jill off using only your imagination at least half the time.

☛ *A special note regarding pornography:* Every second, 28,258 Internet users in the U.S. are viewing pornography, according to Top Ten Reviews online. There are 68 million search engine requests for porn each day — that's 25 percent of all online search requests![5]

Both boys and girls are being exposed to pornography online at younger and younger ages, often by accident, while playing games, surfing YouTube, or doing homework.

Pornography is designed to sexually excite people; this is a typical marketing ploy that works very well. Porn does not turn people into perverts or monsters, but it does have an impact on the ways in which we look at (and operate in) the world. Viewing pornography on a regular basis can have harmful and damaging effects, especially during adolescence when we are forming our ideas of who we are and what we are aroused by.

Pornography
- is a (very poor) substitute for sexual education,
- portrays unrealistic ideas of sexual interaction,
- can distract from actual relationships,
- can lead to negative imprinting to and arousal by unhealthy or illegal things,
- can weaken or atrophy one's own imagination and capacity for fantasy,
- can be addictive,
- can be expensive.

Choosing to incorporate pornography into an existing sexual lifestyle as an adult is very different from constructing a sexual lifestyle built on pornography. Chances are that some of your sexual partners will have used pornography as their primary source of sexual education. Particularly if you date boys, you may encounter some partners who think they know how to "do sex" because they have watched so much porn. However, although the things you see in online pornography are sexual, they are not necessarily actual sex. And some of the things that are actual sex can be considered varsity or olympic-level sex, reserved for adults with much more experience and practice. Do not feel pressured into doing anything you do not want to do.

Kissing

No one seems to be quite clear on how or why touching our lips to someone else's became a big deal. There are many theories; what we do know is that people have been smooching each other for centuries, with references found as early as 1500 B.C.[6]

The modern romantic kiss is one of the few sexualized acts that involves all five senses; sight, sound, smell, touch, and taste. Kissing is also incredibly intimate, feels good, evokes passion, and creates a physical connection between ourselves and our partners.

The basic components of a kiss are eye contact, slightly parted lips, and a tilt of the head so your noses don't hit. (Note: Twice as many people tilt to the right rather than the left.[7])

Putting your tongue into the other person's mouth (or letting them put theirs into yours) is commonly called French kissing or "making out." Learning how to do this, and doing it well, is important. This does not mean wagging your tongue around like a dog out a window or trying to suck someone's ribs up through their neck. The best ratio is one minute of tongue for every three minutes of no tongue. Other tips for kissing:
- Proceed carefully with eyeglasses and braces.
- Fresh breath and a clean mouth are very good things (although two garlics, two coffees, or two orange-mango smoothies generally cancel each other out).
- And smoking is a kissing no-no. You shouldn't be doing that, anyway.

You can catch certain infections as well as the common cold from kissing, but most people agree that kissing is well worth it.

Hickeys are bruises caused by sucking blood to the surface of the skin. The bruising can last from a couple of days to a couple of weeks. Most people give hickeys as a way of marking their territory. Giving hickeys is generally seen as immature, very "middle school," and should never, ever be done to someone without consent or on a place they can't cover up. The social issues that hickeys cause include embarrassment and getting in trouble with your parents or boss. Having a hickey can make you look (very publicly) like someone who does not make good choices, although there is a relatively small percent of the population that thinks hickeys are cool or funny. Don't let those people anywhere near your neck.

Foreplay and Afterplay

All the fun, cute, lovey, rubby, gropey stuff you do before and after the actual sex is just as important (and can be just as much fun) as the actual sex. This stuff is called foreplay when it happens before sex, and afterplay when it happens afterward.

Foreplay can range from conversation to cuddling to kissing to contact with more than a dozen pleasure spots on the body. These are called erogenous zones, and they include the genitals, and also many other sensitive areas of the body that can make touching feel very sexy. These areas include
  • the scalp, hair, ears, and lips
  • the neck and collar bone
  • shoulders, underarms, and wrists
  • nipples (yes, even on the boys)
  • belly buttons, hips, and lower back
  • perineum (the small area between his testicles and his anus — also called the "taint")
  • testicles
  • toes and the backs of the knees

Take your time. Mix it up, and try to find a new zone. Ask questions — everyone's body and response are different.

☛ *A special note about foreplay:* When a penis is ready for sex, it is obvious, and it happens quite quickly. This is not true for women. A vagina can take quite a bit more time to get wet than it takes for a penis to get hard. This is hard (no pun intended) for some guys to understand. Don't be afraid to encourage your male partners to be patient, check in, ask you questions, and help you along.

Anuses do not have the natural lubrication that vaginas do, so even more time and prep is needed before someone's butt is ready for sex (see Chapter 10).

Manual (that means your fingers) and oral (that means your mouth) sex can play a big part in foreplay. A lot of woman report having an easier and more pleasurable time with intercourse if they have already had an orgasm some other way. Remember, many people (more women than men) can have more than one, although most guys may only have one good one in them per day. Again, some boys may need to have this explained.

Afterplay does not need to last nearly as long as foreplay, but it is a great way to express the range of feelings that can happen after two people have sex with each other. Kissing or talking can help you communicate thoughts and feelings that are harder to say in other situations. That said, turning on the TV, grabbing a snack, or spending a few minutes cuddling before falling asleep can be nice, too.

CHAPTER 8
Oral Sex

Oral sex is when one person puts their mouth or tongue on the genitals of another.

When this is done on a woman, it's called **cunnilingus**, or is sometimes referred to as "eating her out" — even though there is no actual biting involved.

When performed on a male, oral sex is called **fellatio**, or is more typically called a "blow job" — even though there is no actual blowing involved.

Guidelines for performing oral sex on a guy:
- No teeth!
- Don't be afraid to use your hands.
- Think ice cream cone, not banana.
- Deep-throating (when someone takes someone else's entire penis into their mouth and throat) is a porn thing. It is varsity-level stuff, and takes specialized training and/or practice. It rarely ends well in real life. A lapful of whatever someone had for lunch earlier is not sexy. Do not try.
- Don't forget the testicles. Jiggle (don't squeeze) them, tug (don't pull) them, and stroke (like the top of a cat's tail, not the back of a dog's ear) them.

Guidelines for performing oral sex on a girl:
- Do not go straight for the clitoris.
- Tongues hurt unless they are lubricated.
- Do not wag your tongue about like a dog out a window.
- Spelling the alphabet with your tongue (or her name ... or the lyrics to your favorite tune) is fun for everyone.
- Use your fingers, as long as your nails are short and clean.
- Keep your nails short and clean.

For everyone:
- Ask for feedback.
- Give feedback.
- Reciprocate. Do not ask anyone to put their mouth anywhere that you are not willing to put yours.
- Condoms and other dams are a good idea (see page 88).

Boys tend to like it a bit harder and faster as they get closer to the finish line. Girls tend to like the Exact. Same. Thing.

CHAPTER 9
Vaginal Sex ('PIV')

Penis-in-vagina ("PIV") sex involves a man and a woman moving so that his erect penis goes in and out of her lubricated vagina. PIV can be done from several positions; face to face is the most common, and is referred to as the missionary position. Either person can be on top.

When he is on top, he is often supporting his own weight with his arms, while she lies underneath him with her knees bent or wrapped around him. This allows for both people to negotiate the depth of penetration, as well as allowing his pubic bone to rub against hers, (hopefully) stimulating her clitoris.

This position does not need to be considered standard, but it is popular, mostly because this particular position gives the most amount of skin-to-skin contact, and allows for both eye contact and the ability to kiss. It's also the one seen most often on television and in movies.

This position is also the best for couples trying to get pregnant, because the deep penetration helps the sperm reach the cervix, while her lying on her back helps the semen pool around the opening of the cervix, making it more likely that sperm will enter. This position is also helpful for her because she can relax in a way she can't with other positions.

When she is on top, she can better control the depth of penetration and can also help his penis hit her G-spot. This position allows her to masturbate herself while being penetrated. Most women require clitoral stimulation as well as penetration to achieve orgasm during vaginal sex.[1]

Despite what movies lead us to believe, it is not necessary to orgasm at the same time as your partner, which is sometimes difficult to do, anyway. That being said, PIV, like most sex acts, should be safe and pleasurable for both people involved. Ask questions along the way, and listen to what your partner says. Just because they may be on top of you does not mean you are not the one in charge.

CHAPTER 10
Anal Sex ('PIB')

Penis-in-butt ("PIB") sex is when a guy puts his penis into the anus of another man or a woman. Anal sex is not a gay thing. Statistically, only 50–80 percent of gay guys engage in anal sex.[1] According to the National Survey of Family Growth, it is a regular feature in approximately one-third of heterosexual couples.[2]

A 2008 study out of the Bradley Hasbro Children's Research Center found that more than half of fifteen- to nineteen-year-olds have oral sex, and that anal sex is increasing among straight teenagers and young adults (in fact, between 1995 and 2004, it doubled). Straight kids participate in anal sex to avoid pregnancy, to please a partner, or to preserve their virginity (this is called "saddlebacking"[3]).

☛ *A special note about saddlebacking:* Just to be clear, anal sex and oral sex are still sex. Notice how they both have the word "sex" in the name? Even if you leave the word "sex" off and say things like, "I got oral last night" or "We did anal last weekend," it still counts as sex.

Anal sex and oral sex are still sex.

Chapter 11 discusses the concept of virginity, and what a fluid, customized, and complicated concept it can be, but if you are actively having oral or anal sex in order to still consider yourself a virgin, you are not going at sex and sexuality like a grown-up.

During PIB, in general, the person being penetrated during anal sex is referred to as the "bottom." The penetrator is the "top." There are not many places in the human body with more nerve receptors than the anus, so anal play can feel good to some people.

Along those same lines, guys have prostates. The prostate is that mini-doughnut-like gland about 3 inches inside a guy's butt and toward the front wall (towards the belly button). When the prostate is bumped by a finger, penis, or some other object, it makes anal sex very pleasurable,[4] and many people consider it to be similar to the G-spot in women. Some guys figure this out on their own during masturbation, and some guys choose to do this with other people (either guys or girls).

Girls do not have prostates, although some women enjoy anal sex. Anal sex is best for women when there is clitoral stimulation at the same time.

☛ ***Another note about pornography:*** Porn is not real. Porn is fantasy. Porn is sexual, but it is not sex. Despite what you see in the porn, anal intercourse is not something to be done spontaneously. In real life, most people do not look like the people in porn. Most people do not speak to each other the way people in porn speak. Many people don't do a lot of the stuff that people in porn do, and certainly not in that order!

- Never go from anus to vagina. Hepatitis is a great concern, as are intestinal parasites.
- Along those same lines, never go directly from ass to vagina, either. There is a lot you don't see that happens in between scenes in porn, including showers, loads of hand washing, and sometimes sandwich breaks.

As with oral sex, reciprocation is important. Anyone who wants to stick anything up your butt should be willing to have the same thing done to them. This creates empathy, helping them to be as gentle and safe with you and your parts as they want you to be with them and theirs.

Anal sex is generally more pleasurable for guys than it is for women. When a man is penetrated in some way by a female partner, it is referred to as "pegging." Putting a mouth on someone's anus is called analingus, but is more commonly referred to as "rimming." Any of these acts can be considered fun or gross, or something in between, depending on whom you ask. What some people frown upon, many others enjoy as healthy sexual expression.

And, though these alternatives do avoid the problem of pregnancy, there are still risks:
- The lining of the rectum is thin, easily damaged, and can allow the HIV virus to enter the body.[5]
- The anus is not very well lubricated, so it is important to use some other form of lubricant to make sure that the person being penetrated isn't injured in any way.
- Condoms are more likely to break during anal sex than during vaginal sex.
- The risk of contracting other STIs is higher for anal sex than oral sex.

According to the CDC, the probability of the receptive partner catching HIV during unprotected oral sex with an HIV carrier is one per 10,000 acts. During vaginal sex, it's ten per 10,000 acts. During anal sex, it's fifty per 10,000 acts.

This means that anal sex is five times more dangerous than vaginal sex, and fifty times more dangerous than oral sex.[6] So some safety guidelines are necessary if you are going to try anal sex.

- Go in slowly.
- Go out slowly.
- Ask questions along the way, and tell your partner what you want/ don't want.
- If you think it's going to hurt, it will.
- Relaxation is not the only requirement for a good experience. Taking your time, being gentle, and using plenty of lube helps avoid both the pain and trauma that can result from improperly attempted anal sex.
- Stretching is a big part of the prep. Start with fingers first.
- Use nothing sharp, including and especially fingernails.
- Make sure anything that goes in will come out.
- Stop when there is pain.
- The bottom (the one being penetrated) is the one in charge.

☞ ***A special note about lubrication:*** Vaginas produce their own natural lubricating fluids. The amount and effectiveness of each woman's lubrication varies throughout their lifetime, and their monthly cycle, but the fluid they produce makes penetration easier.

Anuses are not self-lubricating, and anal sex without the addition of a lubricant can be very painful. It also greatly increases the risk of damage to the lining of the rectum, as well as condom breakage. Some lubes are specifically designed for anal sex. Look for water-based lubes with just a touch of silicone.

There are four main types of lubrication. **Glycerin lubes** are water-based, which means that they can be washed off with water, and when they dry out, they can be reconstituted with water as well. Glycerin dries fast and absorbs into the skin, so these lubes need to be reapplied or reconstituted often. The sugars in glycerin can contribute to yeast infections in women and should not be used if you are diabetic or if your immune system is compromised. Glycerin does not stain sheets or eat away at condoms, but glycerin is an ingredient in laxatives, so do not use it for anal sex, because ... yeah.

Silicone lubes are a less sticky and longer-lasting form of water-based lube, because the silicone prevents the lube from drying out. Most lubricated condoms are made with silicone. Not all silicone lubes are condom safe, although most are; check for a label that says "CE." Silicone cleans up with soap and water.

Natural oils are typically plant- or vegetable-based and safe to eat, which means they are safe to put inside your body; however, *they will destroy condoms*. These are best saved for massages and masturbation.

Petroleum-based lubes are oil-based, synthetic (artificial), and not digestible. They can also cause irritation inside vaginas and anuses, destroy condoms (making the spread of disease easier), and they don't have any antibacterial properties. These lubes include things like Vaseline, lotions, or hair conditioners. Don't use these for sex.

Other general guidelines for lubes:
- Anything with oil in it will destroy a condom.
- In general, avoid lubes with scent, comical pictures, and silly phrases.
- Any lubricant that contains the ingredients lidocaine or benzocaine should be avoided. These chemicals are desensitizers, reducing your body's ability to feel pain, increasing the likelihood of damage and infection.

☞ *A special note about nonoxynol-9:* In the past decade, there has been a growing body of evidence showing that nonoxynol-9 should not be used for vaginal or anal sex.

Nonoxynol-9 can kill both sperm and HIV, but it also causes irritation to the vaginal and anal walls, making it easier for HIV (and other diseases) to be transmitted through abrasions. Because of this, many HIV, AIDS, and health organizations — including the CDC and the World Health Organization — have called for the sale of condoms that contain nonoxynol-9 to be discontinued.[7]

Unfortunately, nonoxynol-9 is the most popular spermicide in the U.S. You may not want to give up the (slight) anti-pregnancy benefit during vaginal sex — or you may not think that the benefit is big enough to risk the possible damage by irritation. The choice is yours regarding vaginal sex; nonoxynol-9 should never be used for anal sex.

Abstinence

Abstinence means not doing something. It could apply to lots of things, but in this context, we are talking about sex.

Choosing to be abstinent from sex and sexual play with other people is the only sure method of avoiding STIs and preventing an unplanned pregnancy. Short of abstinence, masturbation (sex by yourself) is considered safe sex. Monogamy — sex with only one other person within a committed long-term relationship — with someone who has tested free of any STIs is also generally considered to be safe sex, but it can lead to pregnancy.

There are many ways in which you can give and receive sexual pleasure without having sexual intercourse. Fondling, kissing, and hugging can be a way of sharing and showing loving and sexual feelings for each other. For some people (and at some times), these kinds of activities can be more fulfilling than sexual intercourse.

Some people decide that they do not want to start having sex until they are in a significant or long-term relationship. Some decide to wait for marriage, or college, or prom, or Friday. The decision to abstain from sexual behavior can either be long term or short term.

It is important to know and trust yourself enough to decide if something is not the right thing for you at a particular time. It is also important to understand that you will someday meet someone you want to have sex with, and you need to be prepared. You are only abstinent until you decide not to be.

☛ *A special note about abstinence contracts:* Research from four cycles of the National Survey of Family Growth, which studies information on sexual and marital behaviors, reports that almost all Americans have sex before marrying. According to the research, this behavior is the norm in the U.S., and has been for the past fifty years. A 2007 study published in *Public Health Reports* shows that by age twenty, 75 percent of Americans have had nonmarital sex. That number rises to 95 percent by age forty-four.[1]

Most people who vow to save themselves for marriage do not. When people make these vows, they sometimes make the mistake of not educating themselves to be prepared for when they do decide to engage in sexual contact. Thinking, "That doesn't apply to me" leads to higher risks of pregnancy and disease. Will you be prepared?

Like swimming, driving, or performing CPR, if you're not doing it right now, it is very important to prepare yourself for later. A Harvard School of Public Health study in 2006, published in *The American Journal of Public Health*, found that teens who made virginity pledges were 52 percent more likely to have sex within a year of making that pledge than teens who did not sign pledges.[2]

Statistically, abstinence vows break four times more often than condoms.[3]

If you decide that what feels right for you is to wait until marriage, don't wear a special bracelet, don't sign your name to a pledge, don't join a club. Just wait.

Anyone practicing abstinence should also be educated and have a backup plan. All that those vows, rings, pins, and clubs do is make you think about sex; more specifically, the sex you are not having. This is the "Cheesecake Rule." If you joined a club that celebrated not eating cheesecake, and you wore a bracelet or ring as a constant reminder to *not eat cheesecake*, would that really help you abstain? Or would it just make you crave cheesecake?

You're probably thinking about cheesecake right now.

By the way, just like no one should force, coerce, or manipulate you into having sex, no one should be making you choose to *not* have sex, either. Abstinence, like indulgence, is a choice. When and if you choose to be abstinent, make sure you are doing it for your own reasons and not someone else's. Part of growing up is learning what (and who, and when) is right for you.

The decision whether or not to remain abstinent should not be something that one has to feel ashamed of making or breaking. Do not let someone intimidate, guilt, force, or otherwise manipulate you into making any decision about your own body. What you do with your genitals is no one's choice but your own.

Virginity

Here's the deal: Virginity is like a candle, not a light bulb. It diminishes with time and experience. It is not turned off or on like a switch. It is also not something one "gives" to or "takes" from another person.

There is no "V card." It's a whole deck, with dozens of little virginities along the way. There is the traditional and literal "virginity" — when you've never had sexual intercourse. But there are dozens of other physical and emotional types of virginity, too, like your first crush, first kiss, first naked time with another human, and first exchange of bodily fluids (which for many people may not be PIV or even penetration).

Overemphasizing one specific act at one specific time can lead people to do things that they do not like or are not right for them. Every new experience and partner can be important, even game-changing, and can bring feelings (both physical and emotional) that you have not felt before.

CHAPTER 12

Deciding What's Right for You

Indulgence, like abstinence and virginity, is a choice. When and if you choose to be sexually active, make sure you are doing it for your own reasons and not someone else's. Part of growing up is learning what (and who and when) is right for you.

Do not let someone intimidate, guilt, force, or manipulate you into making any decision about your own body.

What you do with your own genitals is no one's choice but your own. For all the reasons there are to have sex, there are just as many reasons not to have it. Spirituality, family upbringing, politics, media, our own sense of responsibility, our relationship with ourselves and our bodies, and our knowledge about and comfort level with sex all contribute to our decision about when and how to express our sexuality.

It bears repeating: There is nothing wrong with making yourself feel good or enjoying making someone else feel good, as long as
 • you are comfortable with what you are doing,
 • you are doing it safely,
 • you are doing it legally,
 • you are aware of the consequences,
 • no one (including yourself) is getting hurt.

Things to remember:
 • If you don't feel safe, you shouldn't be doing it.
 • What is safe and mature may not always be what feels best.
 • What feels best may not always be safe or mature (so don't do it).
 • If you can't talk about it, you shouldn't be doing it.

Self-esteem
The way we feel about ourselves is called self-esteem. Low self-esteem can interfere with good decision making. If you need others to fill gaps in your self-esteem, if your self-image depends on what others think of you, or if you think you need to behave in certain ways to earn or keep someone else's love, you may find yourself making choices that are not good for you.

The first time a person has sex should be memorable and important, and can be fun, exciting, and pleasurable. It can also be awkward and even painful. Boys tend to be excited about puberty and look forward to sex; the changes in our bodies feel powerful and fun. Girls, on the other hand, sometimes have a harder time with puberty. The changes in their bodies can make them self-conscious, anxious, and physically uncomfortable. Girls don't generally look forward to sex in the same way boys do.

Many people engage in sex for the first time because they confuse sex with love. They worry that others will think poorly of them if they do not have sex, or think they will like them more if they do.

If you have high self-esteem, you are more likely to make decisions that are safe and right for you. It's a positive feedback loop, because making decisions that are safe and right for you increases your self-esteem.

Some ways to improve your self-esteem are
- hanging out with people who genuinely care about you,
- learning how to give and take compliments,
- avoiding perfectionism,
- setting goals and meeting them,
- exercising,
- getting involved in social activities,
- focusing on things you already know you do well,
- helping others,
- remembering that everybody is different.

There is no clear rule about when someone is ready to have sex with someone else. Ideally, you are ready for sex with someone else when your mind, heart, and crotch are all balanced and working in sync.

But keep in mind:
- Crotches are usually ready before hearts.
- Hearts tend to come online before minds.
- Minds can be taken down relatively easily by hearts and crotches (as well as pot, booze, porn, not enough sleep, too much caffeine, certain songs, other people's crotches, shiny stuff …).
- For most people, the mind, heart, and crotch don't sync up until at least age 16, and sometimes not until 25.

Casual Sex
There are two general flavors of casual sex: **friends with benefits** and **hookups.**

Friends with benefits (FWB) relationships, also known as "benefriends" or "umfriends" (as in, this is my, um ... friend) are sexual but not romantic relationships between otherwise platonic friends.

Reasons people enter these kinds of relationships include
- to explore sex or sexuality with someone they trust,
- to experiment or "learn the ropes" in a safe context,
- just for fun

More negative reasons people become benefriends:
- They hope they can eventually turn it into a romantic relationship.
- They mistakenly think that their body is the most interesting currency they have to exchange in a relationship or get attention.
- They want to get the physical benefits of a dating relationship without any intention of following through on the emotional responsibilities.

FWBs are tricky for a couple of reasons:
- Sometimes, people get emotional (once the sex starts) in ways they did not anticipate, and get weirded-out or uncomfortable trying to stay casual after doing such intimate things with someone.
- When one of the partners becomes sexual with someone else besides their umfriend, there can be issues of loyalty, jealousy, trust, and personal safety (such as the increased risk for STIs).

The keys to a successful, umfriend situation are safety, communication, and balance.
- Follow the same safer sex guidelines that you would in an actual dating relationship.
- Check in regularly to make sure that both people are OK with the nonromantic relationship.
- Do it for reasons that work for everyone. Remember that the most important letter in FWB is the F, not the B.

A successful benefriend situation requires varsity-level maturity, decision making, and communication skills, and should not be taken lightly, despite its perceived casualness. Until you are an actual adult, the most responsible way to view an FWB situation is as legit practice for future dating relationships — not as an alternative to them.

Hookups
FWB relationships are different than hookups. Hookups (or one-night stands) are generally considered sexual interactions that happen spontaneously between people who just met or do not know each other well. Hookups can involve anything

from making out to actual penetrative intercourse, and may or may not be the beginning of an ongoing relationship (though, typically, it is assumed that they are not).

Hookups happen. They are not in and of themselves unhealthy (see Chapter 16), but we are talking about sexual contact without the anchor of relationship, romance, or even respect. So it is important to remember that the chances of someone being harmed both emotionally and physically can increase the more casual your casual sex is.

Before choosing to engage in sex, there are questions to consider, such as:
- Does this feel right?
- Do I know what I am doing?
- Do I know what I want to be doing?
- Do I know the consequences?
- Does this compromise my goals for myself?
- Does this compromise my relationship with my family?
- Does this align with my values?
- Does this compromise my connection to my spirituality?
- Am I ready emotionally?
- Do I want to wait?
- Do I need to be in a relationship to have sex?
- Do I need to have sex to be in a relationship?
- How do I define "sex"?
- How do I define "virginity"?

Another important thing to consider is how your partner answers these same questions. All of these considerations will change as you get older and the world changes around you.

For now:
- Become clear about your wants and needs, and your boundaries and values.
- Know that these may differ from values held by your friends, your family, and your potential partners.
- Be solid with your choices, so you can maintain them when faced with compromising situations or a changing landscape.

☛ *A special note about sex and substances:* Drugs and alcohol interfere with good choices because they disinhibit you. That means they suppress the parts of your brain that control judgment and can cause you to make different choices than you would if you were sober.

It is not a good idea to mix sex and substances for several reasons. When people mix sex and substances, they
- are more likely to forget to use birth control, or use it incorrectly,
- can have a harder time communicating,
- can have a harder time making clear decisions,
- can go further sexually than they want to or planned on,
- can pressure someone else into going further than they want to or planned on.

Most importantly: People cannot legally give or get consent while drunk or high.

Bottom line: If you are too drunk or high to drive a car, you are too drunk or high to drive your genitals.

PART THREE
SEXUAL HEALTH

CHAPTER 13
Sexually Transmitted Infections (STIs)

Currently, there are more than a dozen separate organisms and syndromes classified as sexually transmitted infections.[1] Infections that spread through sexual contact and activity have been known by several names, including "social diseases," "venereal disease" (VD), and "STDs" (sexually transmitted diseases). Most recently, though, the trend has been to refer to them as "STIs" (sexually transmitted infections).

The reason for this is that the word "disease" implies an obvious medical problem, complete with signs and symptoms. But many STIs are caused by bacteria or viruses that do not have clear signs, or have symptoms that can go unnoticed for long periods of times, so the term "infection" is more accurate.

Several STIs, including human papillomavirus (HPV), human immunodeficiency virus (HIV), and chlamydia, can have long-term health ramifications — including infertility, cancer, and death — while exhibiting only the slightest of symptoms.

Important facts about STIs:
- More than 18 million Americans contract an STI each year.[2]
- Nine million of those people are between the ages of fifteen and twenty-five.[3]
- There are 10,000 new diagnoses every day. This averages out to one every eight seconds.[4]
- The CDC estimates that half of all young adults in the U.S. will contract a sexually transmitted infection by age twenty-five.[5]

If you think, or worry, or know that you have been exposed to any STI, follow these three steps:
1. Don't panic.
2. Don't ignore it. Get checked out and treated by a doctor as soon as possible. Taking a friend, partner, or supportive adult with you is also a good idea. A visit to a doctor will provide you with helpful info, a decrease in your stress level, probably a bit of tough love, and some medication, if you need it.
3. Don't have sex again until you're done with step number 2.

Sexually transmitted infections happen. There is no 100 percent safe sex, just as there are no 100 percent safe salad bars or 100 percent safe drivers.

If you do get an infection (and many of you will), do your best to not let it affect your self-esteem. If you are doing due diligence and are responsibly taking precautions, contracting an infection does not make you a bad person any more than food poisoning or fender benders do.

Understanding STIs
The ten big, bad STIs are grouped into the following three categories:
- **bacterial:** gonorrhea, chlamydia, syphilis, and pelvic inflammatory disease
- **parasitic:** crabs (lice and scabies) and trichomoniasis
- **viral:** herpes, hepatitis B, HPV, and HIV/AIDS

That last group — the four H's — are by far the scariest. This class of STI is systemic and includes viral infections that affect organ systems other than just the reproductive system. There are no known cures for these viruses, although there are vaccines to prevent against two of them (see page 78).

The bacterial STIs
Gonorrhea is a microscopic bacterium that spreads via vaginal, anal, and oral intercourse. Gonorrhea causes sterility, arthritis, and heart problems, and a pus-like discharge from the urethra, which causes pain during urination.

Condoms and dental dams offer very good protection against gonorrhea, but both partners can be successfully treated with oral antibiotics. Often, people with gonorrhea also have chlamydia and must be treated for both infections at the same time.

Scary fact: Gonorrhea is one of the most common — and the most invisible — STIs. Eighty percent of the women and 10 percent of the men with gonorrhea show no symptoms,[6] but continue to pass on the infection, causing more than 700,000 new cases of gonorrhea every year.[7]

Chlamydia is a sneaky bacterium that has few symptoms in the beginning, but will cause painful and burning discharges during urination and intercourse, inflammation of the rectum and cervix, swelling of the testicles, bleeding after sex, and, eventually, sterility. It is spread through vaginal and anal intercourse, and there have been cases of passing the parasite from the hand to the eye.

Chlamydia is easily prevented with condoms/dams and (if caught early enough) treated with antibiotics for a week. Chlamydia can be misdiagnosed and confused with gonorrhea.

Scary fact: Most women and half of the men who have this disease do not know that they have it, and are still spreading the disease. Three million American men and women become infected every year.[8]

Syphilis is a sexually transmitted organism (called a spirochete) that causes three phases that go in no particular order, often overlapping and causing different, distinctive symptoms. One phase starts with painless, crater-like sores around your genitals or around your mouth, which ooze a highly infectious liquid. Without antibiotics, a month later, a painful rash appears on your palms and the soles of your feet.

Another phase lasts for years and has no symptoms, which is highly unfortunate because, if left untreated, syphilis progresses to the final phase, which involves hair loss, brain damage, physical disfigurement, paralysis, and death.

Condom use and antibiotics are your best and only defense against syphilis. Damage done during the late stages cannot be undone.

Scary fact: Some people don't think that syphilis still exists.

☞ *A special note about the bacterial STIs:* As of this writing, chlamydia, syphilis, and gonorrhea have risen for the first time in more than a decade, according to the CDC.[9] The highest number of infections is among people in the 15- to 24-year-old range, including two-thirds of all reported cases of chlamydia and gonorrhea.[10] It's likely that if you are reading this book, you fall within that age range.

Because chlamydia and gonorrhea (and one of syphilis' phases) often have no symptoms, many of these bacterial infections go undiagnosed, making it even more dangerous for young people who contract them, and making it easier to spread it to others.

Chlamydia, specifically, has climbed to 1.4 million annual cases in the U.S.[11] This is the highest number of annual cases of any condition ever reported by the CDC. Ever. As in the history of everything, ever.

This is preventable with condoms. As a species, humans have achieved massive breakthroughs in technology and advancement, such as the Internet, artificial hearts, GPS, the Human Genome Project, and Tivo. There is zero reason this should be happening right now.

Due to a host of factors, including the total failure of abstinence-only education, bacterial STIs are likely to continue to (literally) plague the population born after 1990, so the responsibility to stop them falls on your shoulders.

If you're smart enough to read this book and clever enough to download apps that connect you to other humans, then you can find some condoms or dental dams and figure out how to use them (see page 88).

The best ways to avoid contracting and spreading these infections:
- Limit your number of sexual partners.
- Use condoms/dams consistently and correctly. Use a barrier. Every. Single. Time. (Yes, even during blow jobs. That's a thing now — get into it.)
- Set up a regular testing schedule for yourself. Once per year is the minimum requirement to be able to consider yourself a responsible sexually active person. Choose a day for your yearly STI screening, say, August 14 (exactly six months after Valentine's Day, a nice cap to any summer adventures and a fresh start to the school year!). Put it in your calendar app.
  Go ahead, I'll wait.
  Seriously, do it now.
  No, you won't remember later.

Back? Thank you. Now, let's add in a little formula:

For every additional partner you are sexual with throughout the year, cut your time between testing in half. So, two partners per year would mean testing every six months. A third partner would mean getting yourself tested every three months, and so on.

It is also important to remember to ask your clinic to test for all of the major STIs when you get screened. Some clinics do not automatically screen for herpes or HIV, for example, unless you specifically ask.

Pelvic inflammatory disease (PID) is a serious infection that develops when an infection spreads from the vagina and cervix into the reproductive organs. PID is usually the result of a sexually transmitted infection such as chlamydia or gonorrhea. Those infections are spread by vaginal and anal intercourse and, sometimes, oral sex. Insertion and removal of IUDs can increase one's risk for PID as well. If PID is not treated, it can cause serious problems, such as infertility, ectopic pregnancy, and chronic pain.

Condoms offer very good protection against PID. A health care provider can diagnose PID during a pelvic exam. Tests will also be done for chlamydia, gonorrhea, or other infections, because they often cause PID. PID is treated most often with antibiotics and a period of bed rest and abstinence.

Scary fact: In more developed cases of PID, surgery may be needed to repair or remove reproductive organs.

The parasitic STIs

Crabs are also called "pubic lice," "scabies," and "cooties." This is an easily transferred STI that not even barriers can prevent — because these infections are caused by actual bugs. These tiny, gray bugs attach to your skin, turn darker when swollen with blood, and attach eggs to your pubic hair. They resemble tiny crabs, live off of your blood supply, and make you itch like a crazy person.

Treatment consists of a couple of doses of special lice shampoo. The dead crabs (and their eggs) have to be pulled out of your pubes with a tiny comb. Wash clothes, bed sheets, etc. with hot, hot, hot water and some of the shampoo. The only protection against this infection is to limit your number of intimate and sexual contacts, and avoid people who don't. Other things that can help prevent this include washing clothes from used-clothing stores before wearing them, avoiding people who can't stop scratching their crotches, and avoiding sleeping in sheets that do not seem clean — especially if they are on beds of people you don't know very well.

Scary fact: Scabies are a similar bug, but they burrow under your skin instead of clinging to the hair.

Trichomoniasis is caused by the single-celled protozoan parasite, *Trichomonas vaginalis*. The vagina is the most common site of infection, although the urethra in men can also be affected.

Most guys with "trich" do not have signs or symptoms, but some feel irritation inside the penis, discharge with a strong odor, or a slight burning after urination and ejaculation. Symptoms usually appear within one to three weeks of exposure, but the parasite is harder to detect in men than in women.

When someone has been infected, both partners should be treated at the same time to eliminate the parasite. People should avoid sex until both partners finish treatment and have no symptoms. Latex male condoms, when used consistently and correctly, can reduce the risk of transmission.

Scary fact: An infected person (even if that person has never had symptoms or the symptoms have stopped) can continue to infect or reinfect other partners until the infection has been treated.

The viral STIs

Herpes is a virus that takes two forms: simplex 1 and simplex 2. The first one is associated with cold sores or fever blisters. The second type involves hot, itchy blisters that burst open and create ulcers.

Both can be transmitted sexually and start out with flu-like symptoms, followed by a recurring rash, which includes clusters of the tingly sores (simplex 1 on the mouth; simplex 2 "down there," "back there," "under there," and everywhere in between). Once infected, symptoms can be triggered by stress and include painful burning during urination.

Herpes is most contagious from the time when sores appear until the scabs fall off, but some people can be contagious even when they do not have symptoms. Mucous membranes of the mouth, anus, vagina, penis, and the eyes are especially susceptible to infection. One million new cases are diagnosed every year.[12]

Dental dams and condoms help to prevent herpes, but only when the sores are not already present. Medications can decrease the number and intensity of outbreaks, but herpes is not curable, and like many other viruses, remains with you for life. Don't touch anybody anywhere with any part of you that has sores until they heal; wash your hands often; and do not touch the sores.

Scary fact: Sores may be spread from one partner to another, or from one part of the body to another, whenever contact is made.

Hepatitis B (HVB) is a virus that is transmitted sexually and through all bodily fluids. It is very sneaky and very, very, very contagious. In the beginning, it causes extreme fatigue, headache, fever, and vomiting. Later on, symptoms include yellow skin, brown urine, and attacks on the liver, which lead to cirrhosis, cancer, and possibly death. Almost 40,000 Americans get HVB every year (and an estimated 1.2 million people in the U.S. have it right now).[13] **Hepatitis C (HVC)** can be spread by sex as well, but much more rarely, and is more associated with drug and alcohol use.

Barriers offer some protection against HVB and HVC during vaginal, anal, and oral intercourse, but the virus can be passed through kissing and other intimate touching. In some cases, the infection clears up in a couple of months, but some people remain contagious for the rest of their lives. HVB is preventable with a vaccine, but only if you get it before exposure. If you were born before 1991 and/or did not get it as an infant, go and get it. Now.

Scary fact: Hepatitis is more than 100 percent more contagious than HIV.[14]

HPV (genital warts) are cell-mutating human papillomaviruses that come in approximately ninety different varieties and cause a variety of itchy, flesh-colored, cauliflower-like warts. This disease is spread through genital contact, with or without symptoms. There are a few strains of HPV that do not manifest as warts, but that's not good news; these varieties can cause cancers in the cervix, vulva, and penis.

Genital warts can be prevented with dams and condoms, and can be treated with suppression medications, professional freezing, topical creams, lasers, and acids in places you really don't want lasers and acids. A vaccine has been developed (go ask your doctor!), but at this time, there is no cure. Rumor has it that after several years you can "grow out of it," but this has not been proven.

Scary fact: If left untreated, the warts can grow to block the openings of the vagina, anus, urethra, or throat.

HIV (human immunodeficiency virus) is a viral infection that can weaken the body's ability to fight disease and cause acquired immune deficiency syndrome (AIDS) — the last stage of HIV infection. HIV is spread through blood, semen, and vaginal fluids. HIV remains in the body for life and is the most dangerous of all STIs, causing weight loss; constant, uncomfortable diarrhea; purplish growths on the skin; pneumonia; a variety of cancers; and death.

HIV is prevented through condom use and can be managed with drugs. It is incurable, currently fatal, and at this time, no one has recovered.

Scary fact: There may be no symptoms of HIV for ten or more years after the virus is contracted.

☞ *A special note about vaccines:* Two of the most serious STIs now have vaccines available that can help prevent you from becoming infected. The first vaccine is for hepatitis B. Depending on which of two different vaccine types your medical provider carries, a series of two or three shots over a six-month period is given to people between the ages of eleven and eighteen. It has been part of the recommended immunization schedule for babies born after 1991 in the U.S.[15]

It is important to find out if you have received the vaccines because, although HVB is generally considered an adult disease, it is extremely contagious, and underagers can get infected as well. Thanks to the immunization, HVB infections have dropped 95 percent since routine immunization began in the early 1990s,[16] although the CDC estimates that approximately 1 million people in America carry HVB in their blood, and 5,000 people a year die from this virus.[17]

There is also now a vaccine that prevents the types of genital human papillomavirus (HPV) that cause most cases of cervical cancer and genital warts. The vaccine, Gardasil, is given in three shots over six months. The vaccine is routinely recommended for people ages nine to twenty-six, especially if they are sexually active.[18]

It is theoretically possible that, if every young woman can be vaccinated once she becomes sexually active, cervical cancer may be eliminated completely in future generations. But do not be fooled by the assumption that HPV is a girl thing because the vaccine is pushed for teen girls and associated with cervical cancer. A 2011 study from the H. Lee Moffitt Cancer Center and Research Institute reported that half of all American men might be infected with the human papillomavirus.[19] The HPV vaccines are approved for males ages nine to twenty-six as well, and along with condoms, are two of your biggest weapons against HPV.

Our third weapon against HPV is our immune system, which clears most HPV infections with little difficulty. However, the strain HPV-16 is connected to mouth, throat, head, neck, and anal cancers in men. HPV can be spread through oral and anal sex, as well as vaginal sex.

If and when you choose to become sexually active, it's almost guaranteed that you will be exposed to some strain of the nearly 100 different types of HPV (genital warts being one of them). Vaccinating males will benefit them by preventing genital warts and rare cancers, such as penile and anal cancer. It is also possible that vaccinating boys and men will have indirect health benefits for girls and women.

The human immunodeficiency virus (HIV) can infect and live in your body while slowly weakening your immune system, which is your body's mechanism for fighting off infections.

Specifically, HIV attacks a type of white blood cell called the T lymphocyte (or T cell). T cells help defend against infections and diseases. If HIV enters the body, it attacks a T cell and slowly works its way inside the cell. Once inside, the virus takes over and uses the cell as a virus-making factory to copy itself. The newly made viruses then leave the T cell and go on to infect and destroy other T cells. This is how HIV multiplies. Once a T cell has been invaded, it can no longer fight illnesses within the body.

The T cell range in the typical human is between 500 and 1,800 (typically 800–1,200). When a person's T cell count drops below 200, their immune system is considered compromised (too weak to keep them safe from infections). This is called acquired immune deficiency syndrome (AIDS).

AIDS makes us very susceptible to other bacterial and viral infections that we would normally be able to fend off. AIDS doesn't kill you — it makes you die from other things. Even things such as the common cold, which is easily fought off by healthy immune systems, can become very dangerous.

Being infected with HIV and having AIDS are two different things.

Someone who is infected with HIV is called HIV-positive. Being HIV-positive does not necessarily mean that someone will progress to full-blown AIDS. Some people can stay relatively healthy and free of symptoms for several years or even longer with medications that are available today. The term "poz" has been embraced, particularly in the gay community, for people who are HIV-positive.

People are diagnosed with AIDS when they have a very low number of active T cells left and show signs of a serious infection. There are thirty-three AIDS-defining illnesses, called opportunistic infections, which take advantage of weakened immune systems.

Twenty years ago, having AIDS meant that you were dying. Today, the situation is different, thanks to medication regimes that can slow down the virus's progress. However, even though researchers understand the virus more and more each year, AIDS is still considered fatal.

HIV is spread through blood, semen, vaginal secretions, and breast milk, but blood transmission is most common. Transmission occurs when any of these four infected fluids move from one person's body into another's through
- unprotected sex with an infected partner
- sharing needles during drug use
- transmission of fluids from mothers to babies during childbirth or breastfeeding

People who have another sexually transmitted infection, such as syphilis, genital herpes, chlamydia, or gonorrhea are at greater risk for getting HIV during sex if they have an infected partner. Some STIs increase risk because of the presence of sores, but any infection in the body will trigger the immune system to attack with more T cells, which the HIV virus feeds on.

Although an HIV-positive person may look and feel healthy, the virus is silently reproducing itself and destroying more and more T cells. It can take awhile for someone's body to recognize that it is under attack or to show symptoms, which is a major factor in why the disease is still spreading.

Scary fact: Half of all HIV infections in the U.S. occur among persons younger than the age of 25.[1]

It is possible to find HIV in the saliva, tears, sweat, and urine of infected individuals, but there are no recorded cases of infection by these secretions. Animals and insects do not pass on the disease, nor can HIV be transmitted by sharing silverware, water, food, toilet seats, or even hot tubs and swimming pools with infected people.

The CDC reports that latex (or polyurethane) condoms are highly effective in reducing the risk of HIV transmission.[2] The risk is lower for the penetrative partner than the receptive partner (in general). Oral sex has a relatively low risk because of the low pH levels in the mouth and enzymes in saliva that kill HIV. Any anal sex causes microscopic tearing and invisible amounts of blood, which increases the risk of HIV. There are also studies that have shown that HIV can penetrate healthy, intact vaginal lining.

Intravenous drug users should not share needles or injection equipment.

Just as overactive immune systems increase risk of HIV infection, so do compromised systems, so self-care and stress management are important risk-reduction tools as well.

Just because someone is exposed does not mean that they will be infected. Testing is important and best done within three months. Between 90 and 95 percent of infected people will have enough antibodies to show up in a test within the first twenty-five to thirty days after infection; by the three-month mark, almost everyone who is infected will test positive. After that three-month mark, HIV rapid tests can be taken at public health clinics, and results can be obtained in as short a time as twenty minutes.

There are two tests. The first is the enzyme-linked immunosorbent assay (ELISA) test, which screens for antibodies. A negative ELISA test means you are HIV-negative. A positive ELISA test means you need to take a second test, a western blot test, which screens for the virus itself. A person needs a positive response on at least one of these tests to be diagnosed HIV-positive.

After exposure to HIV, there is **post-exposure prophylaxis** (PEP), which is a month-long medication regimen that greatly decreases the likelihood of infection, especially if taken within twenty-four to seventy-two hours of infection. The medications are usually available in emergency rooms, and work by stopping the infection before it reaches the lymph nodes. The meds are extremely hard on the body and quite expensive, ranging from $800 to $2,000 for a month's supply.

Pre-exposure prophylaxis (PrEP) is an anti-HIV medication that keeps HIV-negative people from becoming infected. It is most commonly referred to by its prescription name, Truvada. Truvada can be used in two different ways.[3] Though it can be used in people as young as 12 who have already been exposed to HIV to treat their infection and manage symptoms, it can also be used (along with other safer sex practices, such as condoms) to reduce the risk of being infected with HIV by someone else. Unfortunately, right now it is only approved as a preventive measure for adults (18 and older).[4]

Truvada is a daily pill that has been approved as safe and effective by the FDA. It stops the HIV virus from being able to duplicate itself, interfering with its ability to create an infection. Truvada does not cure HIV or AIDS, but when used properly it has been shown to reduce the risk of HIV infection by as much as 92 percent.[5]

PrEP is a smart option for anyone who is at greater-than-usual risk for contracting HIV. This includes
- anyone who is in an ongoing relationship with an HIV-positive partner;
- anyone who is (or dates) a gay or bisexual man who has had anal sex without a condom or been diagnosed with an STD in the past six months;
- anyone gay or straight (or other) who does not regularly use condoms during sex with partners of unknown HIV status (and who are at substantial risk of HIV infection, e.g., people who inject drugs or have bisexual male partners);
- intravenous drug users.

If you are older than 18 and fall into one of the categories listed above, PrEP may reduce your risk of contracting HIV.[6] Your doctor can give you a prescription or direct you to a medication assistance program.

Whether or not you fall into any of the categories above, always practice safer sex techniques (such as choosing less risky behaviors, consistent testing, communication, and condom use), and never share needles with anyone for any reason.

☛ *A special note about STIs:* The infections I've described in the past two chapters are all gross, upsetting, and/or downright terrifying. Sexually transmitted infections at their best are disgusting and uncomfortable, and at their worst can be life-threatening.

If you think you've been exposed to an STI, or if you are having symptoms that make you worry that you've got one, you owe it to yourself and your partners to see a doctor immediately. There is nothing to be gained by waiting (except possibly a worse diagnosis and more infected teens). If you are old enough to have sex, you are old enough to behave responsibly and face the risks of sex head on. Contracting an STI doesn't make you a bad person, but knowingly or carelessly spreading one does. Get yourself checked out, and get yourself healthy.

Help and support about STIs is available twenty-four hours a day, seven days a week from Planned Parenthood, 800-230-PLAN (7526), *PlannedParenthood.org*.

CHAPTER 15
Contraception and Safer Sex

Contraceptives reduce the likelihood of pregnancy. Safer sex reduces a person's exposure to disease. All sexually active people can benefit from proper and consistent uses of both contraceptives and safer-sex practices.

If you are sexually active and *not* using some form of contraception, you have a 90 percent chance of getting pregnant in the next year.[1]

Contraceptive and safer-sex techniques are not always easy to use or do. They can be hard to talk about, learn about, and remember. They can be complicated, messy, inconvenient, awkward, and not 100 percent effective, even when used properly. In fact, the ideal would be for both partners to use something, such as a condom and birth control pills.

No contraceptive is 100 percent effective — even abstinence, because people change their minds, and may not have educated themselves on other methods. People can also be pressured or forced into having sex.

Knowing that you and your partner are doing everything you can to be safe and protected makes sexual behavior less stressful and more exciting. To do this, your contraceptive and safer-sex method must
- be effective (to avoid pregnancy and disease),
- be safe (to avoid medical consequences),
- fit your personal lifestyle (to avoid being forgotten or used inconsistently),
- do all of the above for your partner.

It's important that you do not place all of the responsibility for protection on your partner. Safer sex is the responsibility of both partners. The stress, responsibility, time, and cost involved should be shared — just like the babies or the bugs would be. Again, each person should be responsible for using birth control.

The Process of Conception
Fertilization usually occurs in the upper third of one of the Fallopian tubes (the oviduct). Thirty minutes after ejaculation, sperm are present in the oviducts, having swum from the vagina, through the uterus, and into the tubes. Of the several hundred million sperm released during ejaculation, only a few thousand reach the egg. Of those few thousand, only one sperm will fertilize the egg, fusing with receptors on the surface of the egg and triggering a series of chemical

changes in the outer membrane that prevent any other sperm from entering the egg. Fusion of the egg and sperm form what is called a zygote.

The uterine lining becomes enlarged and prepared for implantation of the embryo. The lining of the uterus and the embryo then interlock to form the placenta (the nourishing boundary between the mother's system and the embryo's system). The umbilical cord extends from the placenta to the embryo, and transports food to and wastes from the embryo.

The Process of Contraception
The different available techniques for preventing pregnancy each work by stopping one of the three stages of reproduction:
1. release and transport of gametes (the movement of the sperm and egg)
2. fertilization (the fusion of the sperm and egg)
3. implantation (the implanting of the egg in the uterine wall)

Safer sex/contraceptive methods can be grouped into five categories: natural methods, spermicides, barrier methods, hormonal methods, and medical methods.

THE NATURAL METHODS
Natural methods use few, if any, additional devices and rely mostly on cooperation and timing.

Abstinence is choosing not to participate in sexual behavior with other people.

Positives:
  • *No side effects*
  • *Accepted by most religions*

Negatives:
  • *Refraining is difficult to do for some people.*
  • *Abstinence eventually ends for most people.*

Abstinence can be considered approximately 75 percent effective, because approximately one-quarter of teens who practice abstinence become pregnant within one year.[2] Anyone practicing abstinence should be educated in other methods and have a backup plan.

Alternative methods involve the penetration of orifices other than the vagina, such as the mouth and anus.

Positives:
- *Can be incorporated into sex play*
- *Low risk of pregnancy (unless sperm accidentally lands on a woman's vulva)*

Negative:
- *Alternative penetration does not prevent the spread of disease.*

Alternatives can be considered 99 percent effective.[3]

Masturbation is sexually pleasing oneself (or another) using manual techniques, instrumental manipulation, or combinations of these.

Positives:
- *Costs nothing*
- *Can be done quickly and conveniently*
- *Reduces stress*
- *Can be incorporated into sex play*

Negatives:
- *Masturbation is frowned upon by some religions.*

Masturbation can be considered 100 percent effective as both safer sex and birth control.

Rhythm methods are also called "fertility awareness methods" (FAMs). These involve the charting of menstrual cycles in order to predict the approximately nine "unsafe" days on which a woman is most likely to become pregnant. These days are identified by checking temperature, urine, calendars, or changes in cervical mucus.

Positives:
- *No side effects*
- *Calendars, thermometers, and charts are easy to get*
- *Accepted by most religions*

Negatives:
- *Requires frequent (accurate and scheduled) monitoring*
- *Irregular periods, mucus, or temperature changes can make estimation difficult.*

Rhythm methods can be considered 75 percent effective.[4]

THE SPERMICIDES

Spermicides are used to kill sperm, and can be a foam, cream, jelly, film suppository, or tablet placed inside the vagina, blocking sperm from entering the vaginal canal and killing them.

Positives:
- *Is effective immediately after insertion*
- *No hormones are involved*
- *Adds lubrication*

Negatives:
- *Requires a clinician visit*
- *Requires practice*
- *Can irritate membranes*
- *Can be messy*
- *Can have an unpleasant taste*
- *Can be cumbersome to carry*

Spermicides can be considered 75 percent effective.[5]

Contraceptive sponges are soft, disk-shaped devices made of polyurethane foam that contain spermicide. Once moistened to activate the spermicide, the sponge is placed inside the vagina to cover the cervix and prevent pregnancy. It is fitted with a small loop for easy removal and disposal.

Positives:
- *Convenient*
- *Effective for more than one act of intercourse*
- *Effective for as long as twenty-four hours*

Negative:
- *Risk of toxic shock syndrome if left in for more than thirty hours*

Contraceptive sponges can be considered 78–85 percent effective.[6]

THE BARRIER METHODS

The barrier methods prevent the fertilization of a woman's egg by blocking sperm.

Barriers come in a few forms: a custom-fitted, thimble-shaped latex cap (cervical cap); a shallow rubber cup (diaphragm); or a silicone cup attached to the cervix via suction (shield). These cover the cervix to prevent the passage of sperm and are sometimes filled with spermicide.

Positives:
- *Reusable and can last several years*
- *Do not have to be used/maintained every day*
- *Can be left in place for as long as forty-eight hours (barriers require additional spermicide before repeated intercourse)*
- *Nonhormonal alternative method for female contraception*

Negatives:
- *Allergic reaction to latex by some users*
- *Cannot be used during menstruation*
- *Can be messy due to the necessity of spermicide/contraceptive gel*
- *Possible increase of bladder infections*

Cervical barriers can be considered 78–85 percent effective.[7]

Dental dams are ultrathin, often scented latex sheets used during oral sex. They range from 6 by 6 inches to 8 by 12 inches (condoms cut up the side and unrolled can also be used), and placed over the vulva or anus.

Positives:
- *Convenient*
- *Inexpensive*

Negative:
- *Reduces sensitivity*

Dental dams can be considered 85–97 percent effective.[8]

Male condoms are latex coverings placed on the penis to prevent sperm from entering the vagina, anus, or mouth.

Positives:
- *Easy to find/purchase*
- *Can help reduce premature ejaculation*
- *Can be incorporated into sex play*

Negatives:
- *Allergic reaction to latex for some users*
- *Can create a loss of sensation*

• Are less effective when used without hormonal methods

Condoms can be considered 78–85 percent effective.[9]

☛ ***A special note about condoms:*** Condoms are
- the only contraceptives that help prevent both pregnancy and the spread of sexually transmitted diseases (including HIV) when used properly and consistently;
- one of the most reliable methods of birth control when used properly and consistently;
- widely available — you don't need a prescription or a doctor's visit;
- discreet and convenient;
- free of the medical side effects some other birth control methods may have;
- only needed when you are having sex, unlike some other contraceptives that require you use them all of the time;
- inexpensive, typically half the cost of a diaper. You do the math.

If you have unprotected, heterosexual sex, you have a 90 percent chance of getting pregnant. With proper condom use, that drops to almost 2 percent.[10]

Use a condom every time.

☛ ***A special note about condom resistance techniques.*** According to a study at the University of Washington, more than 80 percent of guys have used at least one tactic to convince a partner to not use a condom at some point in their sexual history.

This behavior is not OK.

Not using condoms puts you at higher risk for pregnancy and disease. Additionally, a guy who doesn't want to use condoms with you has likely also not used them with someone else, upping your chances even more of being exposed to something you don't want.

Also, it is about respect.

The most common tactics guys use to avoid wearing a condom are:

1. "I'm clean. I just got tested."

Um, pregnancy. Duh. Not to mention that there are loads of STIs that can be asymptomatic in some men (which means they don't know if they have it unless properly and specifically tested). **Your response:** "Hi, 'Clean/Just Got Tested.' I'm 'Not Pregnant' and plan to stay that way. Here's a condom."

2. "You're so hot, I'm so horny. Let's just do it."

A percentage of guys have attention deficit issues, but sex is not something to be making spontaneous decisions about. Expect that some guys you partner up with are going to be hyper-focused, distracted, unprepared, or just don't seem to have enough blood to run both ends of their body at the same time. Carry your own condoms. **Your response:** "You're right. I am hot. So hurry up and put this condom on."

3. "It feels better without a condom."

It's true, condoms can cut down on some of the sensitivity for some guys. But if the difference between wearing a condom and not wearing a condom was so great, guys would notice a sudden change during the 1.5–3.5 percent of the time that condoms break (and most people do not notice when a condom breaks). **Your response:** "Does wearing a condom feel better than your hand?"

4. "I just don't wanna use a condom."

This is the lazy guy's approach. At best, he is irresponsible. At worst, he's putting you on the spot in the hope you'll let him get his way. This stance indicates that he is childish and childlike around safety. Does he "not wanna" wear seatbelts either? Sunscreen? Definitely do not take the chance on breeding with That Guy. **Your response:** "Well, I do. Take it or leave it."

5. "What, you don't trust me?"

Jackass alert! Do not fall for this. This is purely and simply manipulation. Taking someone's insistence to use a condom as a personal insult is an immature, douche-baggy move. That choice is about you taking care of yourself and has nothing to with him. **Your response:** "I'm a safety girl. This is my rule for myself, it's not about you. Is that a problem?"

Bottom line: Be clear about your policy on protection, be open with your partner about it, and stick to your guns — no exceptions. And That Guy — you know, the one who asks *again* after you've already said no? That Guy gets to go home and have sex with himself.

While having sex with men, remember to check occasionally that the condom is still on. Do this by reaching down and feeling for the condom's ring around the base of his penis.

THE TEN COMMANDMENTS OF CONDOMS

1. Thou shalt put them on before there is any sexual contact.
This means every time. Front or back. Night or day. Because sperm can be present in pre-cum — that clear fluid that sometimes comes out of the tip of his penis when it is hard — and because pregnancy is not the only thing condoms protect against.

2. Thou shalt mind expiration dates.
They are there for a reason: Expired condoms are less effective. If a condom doesn't have an expiration date, or if you can't read it, do not use that condom.

3. Thou shalt choose your condoms responsibly.
Only use condoms with reputable names. Avoid "natural" or "lambskin" or anything with a scent (flavors and colors may be OK). Wearing a condom that is too big is almost as dangerous as not wearing one at all. Make sure he is wearing the condom that fits his penis, not his ego.

4. Thou shalt be nice to your condoms.
Use only water-based or silicone lubricant — nothing with oil of any kind in it. Do not use more than one at a time — no doubling up. Store them in your bag, nightstand, or bathroom, not in cars, wallets, or pockets, where they can be damaged.

5. Thou shalt avoid condoms with spermicide.
Studies have found that condoms with spermicide are not that much more effective for preventing pregnancy than nonspermicidal condoms, but may increase the risk of disease because of irritation that can come from some spermicides (specifically nonoxynol-9).

6. Thou shalt keep them handy.
The more available condoms are, the more likely they will be used.

7. Thou shalt put them on properly.
Be sure to roll them the right way. And if either one of you starts rolling the wrong way, toss that condom and get a fresh one (see #1 re: pre-cum). Pinch the tip to create a pocket. No doubling up, no recycling, no reusing.

8. Thou shalt remove them properly.
Make sure he holds the condom at the base of his penis when withdrawing. And make sure he does that before he goes soft. Remind him to tie it off and throw it away — not to flush it. If he leaves it on the floor, he doesn't get invited back.

9. Thou shalt be generous with your friends.
Because the more available condoms are, the more likely they will be used.

10. Thou shalt practice, practice, practice.
Buying condoms is good practice for being a responsible adult, and a great way to take responsibility for your own sexual health is to know how to put a condom on properly (just in case he doesn't).

Here's what to do if a condom comes off or breaks during sex:
- Do not panic.
- Inform your partner immediately.
- Find access to emergency contraception within the first seventy-two hours.
- Get tested.

Here's what to do if someone takes off a condom during sex without telling you:
- Do not panic.
- Find access to emergency contraception within the first seventy-two hours.
- Get tested.
- Do not continue to date or trust That Guy. Any form of nonconsensual sex can fall under the definition of rape.
- You also have the option of calling the police.

Female condoms are a longer, wider form of male condoms, inserted into the vagina or rectum, and held in place with bendable rings at both ends.

Positives:
- *Easy to find/purchase*
- *Can be used as part of sex play*
- *Erections are unnecessary to keep in place*
- *Will not cause latex allergies*

Negatives:
- *Sometimes noisy or irritating*
- *Outer ring can be accidentally pushed inside*

Female condoms can be considered 78–85 percent effective.[11]

Outercourse is sex with clothes on and sex that avoids penetration of any kind (also called "dry sex" or "dry humping").

Positives:
- *No side effects*
- *No preparation necessary*
- *May enhance orgasm later*

Negatives:
- *Relies on self-control and is difficult for some people*
- *Pregnancy can still occur if any sperm land on a woman's vulva.*
- *Dry sex does not prevent against disease when clothing is removed.*

Outercourse can be considered 99 percent effective.[12]

THE HORMONAL METHODS

Hormonal methods stop ovulation and prevent the possibility of fertilization by thickening the woman's cervical mucus, making penetration of the uterus by sperm more difficult, or by altering the lining of the uterus so that the fertilized egg has difficulty implanting.

The birth control pill is a pill of either progestin or estrogen hormone, taken once a day. Both kinds of pills help thicken cervical mucus, which prevents sperm from getting through, and prevent fertilized eggs from implanting in the uterus. There is also a combination pill, which prevents the eggs from releasing. Seasonale, a ninety-one-day regimen (twelve weeks of active pills followed by one week of inactive pills), reduces periods to approximately four per year.

Positive:
   • *Periods become more regular and less severe.*

Negatives:
   • *Pills must be taken daily.*
   • *Side effects such as weight change, depression, nausea, and breast tenderness are common, as are other health risks.*
   • *Health risks increase for smokers or those who are overweight.*

The pill can be considered 91–98 percent effective.[13]

The patch is a slow-releasing hormonal patch (brand name Ortho Evra), which is placed on a woman's body (anywhere but the breast) and prevents fertilization and implantation of eggs. The patch is worn every day and changed weekly (with the exception of one week per month when no patch is necessary).

Positive:
   • *Convenient*

Negative:
   • *Patches may move, accidentally be removed, or be unsightly.*

The patch can be considered 91–98 percent effective.[14]

The shot is a hormonal birth-control injection, available in two types, which prevents the releasing and joining of eggs, as well as the implantation of fertilized eggs. Shots of Lunelle are given once per month, and injections of Depo-Provera are given once every three months.

Positives:
- *Can be effective for as long as three months*
- *Reduces cramps*
- *Convenient*

Negatives:
- *Side effects can include irregular bleeding, headaches, and emotional changes.*
- *It can take as long as the three months to reverse the effects.*

The shot can be considered 91–98 percent effective.[15]

The vaginal ring (NuvaRing) is a combination of a pill and a cervical cap in the form of a bendable, 2-inch plastic ring worn around the cervix for three weeks each month.

Positives:
- *Discreet*
- *Convenient*
- *Placement does not need to be exact*

Negatives:
- *The ring can cause vaginal irritation and discharge.*
- *Physical risks can include worsening diabetes and high blood pressure, and can increase risk for heart attack and stroke.*
- *If the ring remains out for more than three hours, another birth control method must be used until the ring has been used continuously for seven days.*

The vaginal ring can be considered 91–98 percent effective.[16]

Intrauterine devices (IUD/IUS) are small, plastic, T-shaped objects inserted into the woman's uterus. They contain either copper (also known as an intrauterine device or IUD) or hormones (also known as intrauterine system, IUS, or by the brand name Mirena), both of which help prevent the fertilization and implantation of eggs.

Positives:
- *Can be left in place from one (IUS) to twelve (IUD) years*
- *Helps reduce cramping (IUS)*

Negatives:
- *Can increase cramps (IUDs)*
- *Can result in heavier and longer periods.*

Intrauterine devices can be considered 99 percent effective.[17]

The implant, Implanon, is a small plastic rod that is inserted under the skin of a woman's arm, where it releases progestin, helping to prevent the fertilization and implantation of eggs.

Positives:
- *Can be left in for as long as three years*
- *Ability to become pregnant returns relatively quickly after removal*

Negatives:
- *Slight scarring*
- *Irregular and unpredictable menstrual periods*
- *Certain medications (and possibly being overweight) can make the implant less effective*

Contraceptive implants can be considered 99 percent effective.[18]

☛ ***A special note about LARC:*** Long-acting, reversible contraception (or LARC), includes intrauterine devices and contraceptive implants. When choosing contraceptive methods, LARC should be considered safe and appropriate. LARC methods (with failure rates of less than 1 percent per year for perfect and typical use[19]) are highly effective, and have the highest rates of satisfaction and lowest rates of pregnancy of all reversible contraception.[20]

ECPs (emergency contraceptive pills) are also called "Plan B." These are two increased doses of estrogen and progestin taken twelve hours apart and within seventy-two hours of intercourse to thicken mucus and prevent the release of eggs.

They are used by some as a backup when other means of contraception have failed. For example, if a woman has forgotten to take a birth control pill or when a condom tears during sex. It is also a first line of treatment for victims of sexual assault.

The term "morning-after pill" is a misnomer that is falling out of use because of the fact that these pills are licensed for use up to seventy-two hours after sexual intercourse. "Emergency contraception" is the term preferred by the medical community.

Unlike forms of chemical abortion, emergency contraception does not end pregnancies and will not harm a developing embryo. ECPs are not to be confused with chemical abortion drugs such as mifepristone (formerly called RU-486, and also called Mifeprex), which act after implantation has occurred. RU-486 will induce abortion in the first forty-nine days (approximately nine weeks) of gestation using medication rather than surgery. It acts by blocking the hormone progesterone, which is essential for maintaining a pregnancy.

ECPs are not effective as an ongoing method of contraception. They also do not protect against sexually transmitted infections. If a woman takes the drug after the egg has already been released, it won't stave off fertilization or end a pregnancy. The pill must be taken before implantation or it will have no effect. On day one, 95 percent of pregnancies are prevented, compared with 85 percent on the second day, and 60 percent for those starting on the third day.[21]

THE MEDICAL METHODS
Surgical sterilization for men involves a doctor severing the tubes that carry sperm (vasectomy), and for women, the severing of the tubes in which the sperm and egg meet (tubal ligation). Small, nonsurgical metallic implants (called Essure) are also available for women. These are inserted into the fallopian tubes to block pregnancy by building up scar tissue.

Positives:
- *Permanent*
- *No lasting side effects*

Negatives:
- *Mild bleeding after surgery*
- *Difficult to reverse*
- *Does not protect against disease*

Sterilization can be considered 99 percent effective.[22]

Abortion means ending the life of a developing fetus via a number of techniques. Although many abortions are used as birth control, this is not a mature or responsible approach to sex. Abortion is by no means a contraceptive and should not be considered as such.

Positive:
- *Can be used when there are serious health concerns for the mother or fetus, in response to pregnancy arising from sexual abuse or unwanted sex, or in the event*

of ineffective or improperly used birth control

Negatives:
- *Can be both physically and psychologically damaging in possibly life-altering ways*
- *Does not protect against disease*

Abortion can be considered 100 percent effective.[23]

☛ ***A special note about abortion:*** The national rates of unintended pregnancy and abortion declined with the rise of contraceptive use in the 1980s. One million legal abortions are performed in the U.S. every year.[24]

There are three different types of abortion. One is called vacuum aspiration. This is usually done within the first twelve weeks of pregnancy. A thin tube is inserted through the cervix and into the uterus, and the contents are suctioned out.

If the pregnancy has gone past twelve weeks, (but no more than twenty-four weeks), a second method called dilation and evacuation (D&E) is possible. The cervix is opened (dilated) and a small, spoon-like instrument (a curette) is used to scrape the walls of the uterus, then suction is used to clear (evacuate) the uterus.

There is also a third method, the medicinal abortion, with a pill called mifepristone (formerly called RU-486). This involves two pills taken three days apart. The pills induce the woman's body to terminate the pregnancy and clear her uterus. This is done at home up through the seventh week of pregnancy and requires a follow-up visit to her practitioner a few days later to ensure that the abortion was completed.

While abortion is legal in the U.S., physicians who perform abortions are restricted by the regulations of their state's medical association. Most states do not permit abortions after twenty or twenty-one weeks of gestation (pregnancy) unless the woman's health or life is seriously at risk.[25] In some states, you cannot get an abortion without parental consent (permission from a parent if you are a minor) or parental notification (having to tell a parent — but not get that parent's permission — if you are a minor). If you have questions about the rules in your state, call a local, recognized, and legitimate clinic.

Abortions should be performed only by qualified doctors. When done by a responsible practitioner, abortion is safe, especially when done within the first thirteen weeks of pregnancy.

Abortion is safe — but it is not easy.

Abortion is a serious decision. It should not be considered a primary method of birth control. Abortion should be a last resort, used only after other safer-sex methods have been tried (or one of them has failed). Using abortion as a primary method of birth control should be considered irresponsible.

Prevention
Because contraceptives are the best protection we have against most STIs and pregnancy, it is important to use them every time you have sex.

Prevention means
- using protection every time;
- getting tested regularly (and insisting that your partners do as well);
- not having sex under the influence of substances;
- telling sexual partners before the pants come off if you have — or even suspect you may have — an STI of any kind;
- being open and honest with your partners, and willing to have difficult conversations.

It is important to have a healthy, working relationship with your body; to not be afraid of it, and to ask questions when something seems amiss. This is especially important if you are worried that you have been exposed to an STI or may have gotten someone pregnant.

☞ *A special note about STIs:* Practicing safer sex, including getting checked for STIs, is part of responsible sexuality. This is done by making an appointment with your doctor (or local sexual health center) to discuss birth control, tests, treatment for sexually transmitted infections, and other information about your sexual health.

If you find out after being tested that you have an STI, it is very important to avoid accusing, blaming, or ruining others' reputations. Some people make bad choices, but catching something is not uncommon, and many infections do not have clear signs and symptoms, so they can be passed from person to person without carriers knowing they are doing so. If other people were cool enough to let you see them naked and do fun things with them, then it is the polite thing to do to give them the benefit of the doubt and a little respect until you are sure.

It is also very important to let any partners you've had since your last testing know you have an STI. Failing to tell previous partners that they may have been exposed to something not only jeopardizes their health, but also could lead to them infecting others (and it makes you look like a jerk).

Pregnancy

If you think you might be pregnant, do not panic. Follow these steps:

1. Breathe in through your nose and out through your mouth slowly while asking yourself these questions:

   Did someone with a penis ejaculate directly on your vulva, near your vulva (such as your anus), or in your vagina?

   Did the person not wear a condom?

   Is there a chance the condom was used improperly, leaked, or broke?

2. If you answered yes to any of those questions, a pregnancy test should be taken.

3. If you were using a second method of protection at the time (such as the pill or an IUD), your chances of being pregnant are much lower, but you should take a pregnancy test anyway.

4. Tell a responsible adult (this may or may not be your parent(s)) or a friend who cares (this may or may not be your sexual partner).

5. Consider emergency contraception. If it has been less than three days, emergency contraception can reduce the risk of pregnancy.[26] The chances of it working successfully drop with every day that passes, but emergency contraceptive pills can be obtained from your doctor, many pharmacies, emergency rooms, and health clinics. Depending on your age and location, a prescription may be needed.

6. If it has been more than three days or emergency contraception has already been taken, a pregnancy test should still be done.

Remember to keep breathing. They are called pregnancy *scares* for a reason.

There are several signs that may indicate you have gotten pregnant, such as bloating, nausea, sore nipples, hunger, sleep shifts, missed periods, and having to pee a lot more than usual. But these are not certain indicators, as not all will be experienced by everyone; most of them can be caused by something other than pregnancy, and even when they are tied to a pregnancy, usually won't show up for several weeks.

A pregnancy test is the only sure way to know if you are pregnant. The most reliable ones are done in your doctor's office or at a clinic such as your local Planned Parenthood, but home pregnancy tests are also very reliable and can be purchased at any drug store. They are most reliable around a week after a missed period and three weeks after a risk event occurs, but can be taken as early as ten days after a risk event or a soon as you realize your period is late (although results may not be as reliable).

If or when you take a pregnancy test:
- Have someone with you.
- Use a brand-name test.
- Buy more than one (in case you want a second opinion or screw it up the first time).
- Mind the expiration dates on the box.
- Read all the instructions before taking the test.

Tests are considered "positive" if pregnant, and "negative" if not pregnant. False positives (a test that says you are pregnant when you are not) are quite rare. False negatives (saying you are not pregnant when you actually are) are more common due to user error.

If you have a negative pregnancy test, but it has been less than three weeks since the risk event or you have definitely missed a period, another test should be taken (do not reuse a test). Also, you should make an appointment with your doctor or local health clinic within the next week.

If you have a positive pregnancy test, you should schedule a visit to your doctor to verify the results as soon as possible. And breathe.

If you find out after testing that you are pregnant, it is important to get support and information. Ideally, you will inform your parent(s) or caregiver(s) and the father, and begin to research your options, which include abortion, adoption, or parenthood. It's very important to avoid judging yourself too harshly.

Help and support for a pregnancy or suspected pregnancy, and information about options are available twenty-four hours a day, seven days a week:
- American Pregnancy Helpline: 866-942-6466, *thehelpline.org*
- Planned Parenthood: 800-230-PLAN (7526), *plannedparenthood.org*

CHAPTER 16
Responsibility

There are seven crucial criteria that need to be met in order for a sexual interaction to be considered responsible.

The Seven Crucial Criteria of Responsible Sex

1. Privacy
2. Consent
3. Age appropriateness
4. Foreplay
5. Safer sex
6. Afterplay
7. The Big R's

Privacy
Despite our culture's love of reality TV, a lot of people get squicked out when they see people having sex in public. (And the ones who don't get squicked out, you probably don't want watching you anyway!) Plus, it's illegal almost everywhere.

Consent
Consent can be defined as an informed, mutual, sober, honest, understood, and revisited agreement. It is both persons' responsibility to give and obtain clear consent.

The Rules of Consent:

It must be informed. Terms like "hook up," "sex," and "doing it" mean different things to different people. If you can't talk about it, you shouldn't be doing it.

It must be mutual. Equality is key. People too far below your age range, development, mentality, or authority level cannot legally give consent.

It must be sober. If you are too drunk to drive a car, you are too drunk to drive your genitals. Drunk, high, or sleeping people can't give consent.

It must be honest. True consent cannot be manipulated. A "yes" after twenty minutes of whining, guilting, bugging, or begging is not actually a "yes."

It must be understood. Consent is not just about getting a "yes." Consent also means people get to say "no." The absence of "no" does not mean the answer is "Yes." If you are unsure, ask. When you say "no," say it clearly; no "ums" and no giggling.

It must be revisited. Consent is a process, not a goal. For the next level, the next day, the next date ... you and they need to ask again. Giving consent once does not mean you can't say "no" later. Even if you are in a relationship with someone or you've let them do stuff before, they still need to ask each time. People get to say "no" anytime — even if they've already said "yes."

Bottom line: It is illegal — not to mention unethical and reprehensible — to have sex without consent.

Age appropriateness

The state or region in which you live most likely has specific guidelines on the age of consent. It is wise to be aware of these before you choose to engage in sexual activity. (It is also a good idea to research the laws of other states, regions, and countries when you move or are traveling, because nothing can ruin that trip to LA, your freshman year in college, that semester in Spain, or summer at Grandma's beach house like a felony.)

For those of you still in high school, here are good general guidelines:
- Limit all sexual activities to people within two years of your own age.
- Limit your sexual activities to non-penetrative acts until age sixteen.
- Reserve "varsity level" sex acts for people whom you know well, have ongoing caring feelings for, who are willing, and who are insistent on safer-sex practices.

Once you are older than the age of eighteen, "the age rule" kicks in and will be applicable for the rest of your life:
1. Take your age.
2. Divide it in half.
3. Add nine.
4. Do not have sex with people younger than the answer.

This simple equation will help to ensure that you engage in sexual/romantic relationships with people in your general cohort. As we get older, age differences become less important. For example, a forty-two-year-old's and a thirty-eight-year-old's lives probably don't look that different. Likewise, a twenty-nine-year-old and a twenty-six-year-old are probably going through the same general life stages. However, a twenty-two-year-old's and a twenty-year-old's lives should look and feel very different. Even a nineteen-year-old and an eighteen-year-old are potentially living very different lives, especially if one has moved out of his parents' house or started college, while the other is still in high school.

NOTE: Though it can be tempting to be vague or less than honest about your age when dating other people, it can cause a lot of problems. When a younger person lies about their age and gets involved with an older person, it is the older person who can get into massive trouble, including legal charges. Be cool and don't risk anyone else's reputation or freedom by not being yourself.

Foreplay

Foreplay is important for getting your partner ready for sex. Read more about foreplay on page 56.

Safer sex

Safer sex is on this list for obvious reasons; sex cannot be considered responsible without safer-sex methods firmly in place. See page 84.

Afterplay

This is important for communication and caring. See page 56 for more.

The Big R's

These are **respect, relationship,** and **reciprocation.** Sexual morality is not about when you are allowed to have sex; it is about how you treat people when you are in sexual contact with them.

There is no realistic way to make a list of rules that will apply and be useful to all people in all situations, cultures, times, or places. This is why it is important to act with **respect.**

Many of you will have sex with someone along the way that you are not in love with. But as long as you have some kind of **relationship** with them, that might be OK. There may be hookups, benefriend situations, or even sexual relationships that turn into romantic ones.

One-night stands happen (see page 68). Hookups don't automatically equal "unhealthy"; however, **reciprocity** (the third big R) still needs to happen if they are to be considered healthy. Reciprocity is another word for balance or fairness. For example, if one partner is having a one-night stand, but the other thinks it is the beginning of something bigger, that is a problem.

The Big R's look different to different people in different situations, at different times, and in different cultures. Morality is relative. That means what is OK for some people, in some places, at some times is not OK for, in, or at others.

- Do you cheat?

- Do you have sex with someone who is cheating on someone else?
- Do you tell someone if you have an STI?
- Do you go out with or have sex with someone when it clearly means something more to them than it does to you?
- Do you lie about your age or experience?
- Do you hook up with someone who is drunk?

These questions are important to ask ourselves, because (*spoiler alert!*) **sex is not the biggest, most important, monster-size deal that some people make it out to be.** At times in your life, sexual contact may not even seem like a big deal at all. And you are changed after it happens. Relationships change after it happens. And it's hard to predict how the other person is going to respond.

There is no such thing as casual sex if you go at it from a respectful place; all sexual interactions that involve respect have meaning, whether it be a sweet moment with someone you'll never see again, a chance to learn something you wouldn't have otherwise, the start of something incredible that lasts the rest of your life, or just a fond memory to remember when you're older.

The bottom line is that in order to go at sexual and intimate interactions respectfully, you must
- act in a way that you would want to be treated,
- err on the side of caution,
- avoid knowingly or accidentally doing something that could, would, or might harm someone (including yourself).

How to have a safer, healthy sex life
Pregnancy and HIV and other sexually transmitted infections make sexual involvement a serious decision. Though there are potential benefits, intercourse and other forms of sexual activity also bring potential consequences.

These guidelines will help you avoid the unfortunate social, biological, emotional, and legal consequences that sometimes accompany sexual activity.

Have a relationship with your own body before you share it with others.

- Figure out what feels pleasurable to your body and educate yourself about the ways in which it can be harmed. Work to keep it as healthy as possible. Wash it, examine it, and have it tested.
- Get vaccinated against the infections that you are able to, and get a full STI screening once a year for the others.

- Encourage those you care about to do the same.
- Be clear about your wants and needs, as well as boundaries and values, so you can maintain them when faced with compromising situations or a changing landscape.
- Acknowledge that masturbation is the easiest and safest way to avoid sexually transmitted infections and pregnancy. It's also fun, has loads of health benefits, costs nothing, and doesn't usually take very long.

Understand that abstinence only works until it doesn't.

- Acknowledge that staying above the belt or above the clothes can still be fun, significant, and sexy.
- Know that you will be sexually active someday, and that you can (and might) change your mind about your status as abstinent at any time.
- Work to educate yourself about sex and sexuality, regardless of your current level of sexual activity, so that you are prepared when you do indulge in sexual activity.
- Do not have sex if you don't want to have sex. You don't need abstinence contracts (or pins or T-shirts or clubs).
- Do not feel ashamed about choosing to abstain from sexual behavior.
- Do not feel ashamed about choosing to engage in sexual behavior.
- Whether you choose abstinence or indulgence, do so for your own reasons and not someone else's.
- Do not let anyone intimidate, guilt, force, or otherwise manipulate you into making any decision about your own body.
- Know that **oral sex and anal sex are actually sex,** and act accordingly, using the same care, caution, and decision making as you would with penis-in-vagina or penis-in-butt sex.
- Think of virginity as a candle, not a light bulb; it diminishes with time and experience.
- Believe that what defines you as a sexual person and gives you value as a partner is not defined by what, or who, you have done so much as how you treat others and yourself.

If you can't talk about it, you shouldn't be doing it.

- Be willing to have hard conversations; discuss your sexual history with your partners, and ask your partners about their past sexual behavior.
- Remember that what is safe and mature may not always be what feels best (and what feels best may not always be safe or mature).
- Do not do or say anything electronically that you are not prepared to do or

say in real life.
- Do not use sex as an escape or a weapon, and understand that engaging in sexual activity does not prove that you are an adult, that you are straight (or not), or gay (or not), or cool, or foxy, or that you are loved, or are in love with anyone.

Keep your sexual situations responsible.

- Seek privacy when you are sexually active (both with yourself and with others).
- Familiarize yourself with the laws in the state in which you live, particularly those regarding age of consent.
- Do not lie about your age.
- Make sure your partners are in the same cohort and developmental stage that you are.
- Get proof of your partners' ages. Do not simply take their word for it.
- Likewise, do not take anyone's word on their STI status or their birth-control regimen, and always practice safer-sex techniques.
- Make sure your sexual interactions are characterized by respect, reciprocity, and some degree of relationship.
- Avoid making sexual decisions while under the influence of substances. If you are too drunk or high to drive a car, you are too drunk or high to drive your genitals.
- Apply the same expectation to other people: Do not have sex with drunk or high people and do not let friends hook up when drunk or high.
- Remember that foreplay (all the fun, cute, lovey, rubby, gropy stuff that happens before the sex) is important and can sometimes be just as fun as the sex part.
- Remember that afterplay (all the fun, cute, lovey, rubby, gropy stuff that happens after the sex) is important and can sometimes be just as fun as the sex part.
- Understand that, apart from not having sex and masturbation, condoms are the best protection you have against both STIs and pregnancy, so use them every time you have sex (see The Ten Commandments of Condoms, page 91).
- Do not allow yourself to be pressured into doing anything sexual.
- Never force or pressure anyone else into sexual contact, and always get clear consent from your partners (see The Rules of Consent, page 101).

If and when you choose to become sexually active, it should be only after you have thought through the consequences of your actions, gotten permission from (and discussed it with) your partner, and prepared to participate safely.

CHAPTER 17
Sexual Harassment

Sexual harassment can be defined as any unwelcome attention of a sexual nature. It includes a range of behaviors, from mild transgressions and annoyances to serious abuses. Sexual harassment can — but definitely does not have to — include forced sexual activity.

There are two forms of sexual harassment. The first and most obvious is inappropriate sexual behavior. Many times, this involves failing to gain consent before touching others, or ignoring them when they have clearly not given consent.

Inappropriate behavior can also be about words rather than actions: talking to (or at) someone in a sexual way, especially if they have shown or said that they are not OK with it.

Notice I said "talking at" not "talking with." When conversation or attention is one-sided, it's usually a signal that someone is moving out of the category of appropriateness.

The second form of sexual harassment involves making the general environments in which we live, work, learn, and play uncomfortable for others. This type of harassment is more easily done by mistake. Telling lewd jokes, taking or displaying sexually explicit photos, teasing a classmate or workmate about sexual matters, and telling or posting sexual stories or comments can all be perceived as offensive, degrading, or intimidating.

Remember that if you are behaving in a way that others perceive as harassing, the consequences can be serious. Pay attention to how you are treating people, how others are reacting to you, and when in doubt, ask questions.

Likewise, if someone else is making you feel uncomfortable or harassed, say something — if not to the perpetrator, then to a teacher, a parent, or manager.

CHAPTER 18
Sexual Abuse and Assault

Child sexual abuse can be defined as a violation of trust in a relationship with any or all of the following characteristics:
- unequal power and/or advanced knowledge
- the need for secrecy
- sexualized activity (sexualized, not necessarily sexual)[1]

Whenever one person dominates and exploits a younger person through sexual activity or suggestion, or uses sexual feelings and behavior to degrade, humiliate, control, injure, or misuse the other person, it qualifies as sexual abuse.[2] Sexual abuse can include violations of a position of trust, power, and protection against those who lack an adequately developed emotional, or intellectual "immune system," and it promotes sexual secrecy among the people who are victimized.

Sexual abuse involves direct touching, fondling, and/or intercourse against a person's will. Examples include kissing, oral sex, penetration with objects, genitals or fingers, and masturbation. Use of force is sometimes involved, though this does not mean it is always physical or violent.

Sexual abuse frequently occurs in the context of a relationship. This can be family (such as an older sibling or parental figure), but can also happen in teacher-student, coach-athlete, and boss-employee relationships, too. Sexual abuse is about an unfair balance of power, most often an age difference, but can also involve differences in physical power, emotional power, intellectual power, or social power, along with numerous manipulative techniques such as secrecy, bribery, trickery, lies, and threats.

Sexual abuse
- often causes negative feelings, such as confusion, fear, anger, shame, depression, and worthlessness;
- can potentially cause positive feelings, such as feeling special, appreciated, noticed, and loved, as well as physical pleasure;
- is not necessarily violent. Exposure to pornography, for example, can be considered sexual abuse;
- can be hands on (for example, kissing, touching, penetration) or hands off (such as exposure to sexual body parts or acts, being watched or photographed in vulnerable situations).

The severity of sex crimes is defined depending on the
- level of consent
- ages of the people involved
- relationship between the people involved
- genders of the people involved
- behaviors themselves
- location where the behaviors take place

The prevalence of childhood sexual abuse is remarkably high for both boys and girls. According to the National Center for Missing and Exploited Children, 20 percent of all children are molested before the age of eighteen.[3] Most abuse occurs prior to age sixteen; almost two-thirds occurs before the age of twelve; more than half of that before age six.[4]

In fact, out of every 100 friends you have on Facebook, Instagram, or Snapchat, more than 40 will (statistically) be survivors of sexual abuse.[5]

Examples of the traumatic effects of abuse include
- anxiety/panic attacks
- depression
- distractibility/difficulty concentrating
- guilt/shame
- insomnia
- intimacy issues/loss of trust
- irritability/anger
- loss of self-esteem
- memory loss
- negative body image/eating disorders
- nightmares/flashbacks
- numbness/apathy
- poor choice in future partners/victim mentality
- promiscuity
- self-mutilation/harm
- sexual dysfunction
- shock/denial
- social withdrawal/isolation
- substance abuse
- suicidal ideation/attempts

A child who is abused or made to do sexual things with an adult is never to blame — even if they consented to the abuse at the time, cared about their abuser, or enjoyed parts of it.

Sexual acts during sex offenses are *not* sex. They are abuse.

Sexual Assault

Different from sexual harassment (which is usually verbal or communicated through technology) and abuse (which is usually against younger children), sexual assault is a broader category that can include almost any unwanted sexual contact against anyone of any age, regardless of whether or not it happens within a relationship. This can happen in a relationship (as in the case of date rape), but can also happen when the abused and the abuser do not know each other.

Usually, a sexual assault occurs when someone touches another person's body in a sexual way (even through clothes) without that person's consent or permission. Some acts that fall under the category of sexual assault include forced sexual intercourse (rape), sodomy (oral or anal sexual acts), and molestation (touching).

Sexual assault in any form can be a devastating crime. Assailants can be strangers, acquaintances, friends, or family members. They commit sexual assault by way of manipulation: grooming (doing something the other person likes in order to get the person to go along with it), coercion (doing something the other person doesn't like in order to get the person to go along with it), and violence.

Basically, almost any sexual behavior a person has not consented to and that causes that person to feel uncomfortable, hurt, or scared can be included in the sexual assault category.

The law generally assumes that a person does not consent to sexual contact if she or he is
- forced
- threatened
- tricked
- pressured
- unconscious
- drugged
- under a certain age
- developmentally delayed
- chronically or mentally ill

Examples of assault can include
- someone putting their finger, tongue, mouth, penis, or object into your body when you do not want them to;

- someone touching, fondling, kissing, or making any unwanted contact with your body when you do not want them to;
- someone forcing you to perform oral sex or forcing you to receive oral sex;
- someone forcing you to look at sexually explicit material, or forcing or tricking you to pose for sexually explicit pictures;
- a doctor, nurse, or other health care professional giving you an unnecessary examination or touching your body in an unprofessional, unwarranted, and inappropriate manner.

Since every person and situation is different, victims of sexual assault will respond to an assault in different ways. Many factors can influence a person's response to and recovery from sexual assault, including the

- age and maturity level of the person who was victimized,
- social support network available to the person who was victimized,
- response to the attack by police, medical personnel, and parents,
- offender's relationship to the person who was victimized,
- frequency (how often it happened), severity (the level of violence and injury), and duration (how long it went on) of the assaults.[6]

Some survivors of sexual assault will find ways to recover relatively quickly, while others can feel the lasting effects of their victimization throughout their lifetime. Sexual assault is frightening and traumatic. It is important to understand that when someone is assaulted, it is not their fault. Choices can be taken from anyone, but if we surround ourselves with supportive people — both personal and professional — the effects can be lessened.

Being raped or molested does not make you weak (even if you feel powerless). Although many people who have been raped have difficulty discussing it, it is important for them to talk to someone.

Being raped or molested by someone of the same sex does not make you gay (even if there were parts that may have been enjoyable). Genitals feel good when they are touched; it is as simple as that. Some people can become aroused and even orgasm during manipulated or forced sex acts.

If you have experienced any unwanted sexual contact:
- Say something to someone who will listen — a parent, teacher, counselor, or friend.
- Call the police.
- In the case of assault, do nothing that will change your appearance or the appearance of the place of the assault.

- Do not take a bath or shower, or even wash your hands.
- Get medical attention to check for infections or other injuries.
- Take a change of clothes with you to the hospital.
- Write down as much as you can remember about the attack.

The necessary evidence must be collected immediately; the decision about whether or not to press charges can wait.

CHAPTER 19
Personal Safety

There are things you can do ahead of time to keep yourself safe and lessen the chances of being victimized.

- Be aware that walking alone at night may be dangerous.
- Observe constantly. Do not engage in behaviors that restrict your observation.
- Walk with your head up and a confident stride.
- Stay in well-lit areas.
- Trust your gut. If something feels weird, it probably is. Good men do not walk up quietly behind someone when it is obvious that person is unaware.
- Know your routes. Notice lighting, alleys, abandoned buildings, and street people.
- Try to vary your routine. Don't let your behavior be too predictable.
- If you are alone and worry that you are being followed (or you see a person or group farther down the street that makes you feel uncomfortable), cross the street, walk in another direction, or ask other people walking if you can stay with them for a while. Good men do not feel offended when a female crosses the street.
- When walking to your door or apartment, carry your keys in your hand, ready to use.
- While waiting for public transportation, keep your back against a wall (or pole) so that you cannot be surprised from behind.
- Elevators are safer than stairs, but trust your gut if you are alone and there is someone else in the lift. Good men do not feel offended when a female chooses a different elevator.
- When parking your car, note its location carefully so that you can go directly to it.
- When returning to your car, look around. If you notice anything or anyone suspicious, go back the way you came.
- If you have electric locks, know how to unlock the driver's door only (as opposed to all the doors at the same time).
- If you return to your car and find it parked next to a big van — especially one without side windows — enter your car from the passenger door, or wait and come back later.
- Do not park next to big vans — especially those without side windows.
- As soon as you get into your car, lock the doors and leave.
- Make a habit of not letting your gas indicator fall below the quarter-full mark.
- If you run out of gas or have an accident, don't take rides from strangers. If a stranger wants to help, ask that person to call a repair truck or police officer for you (if you haven't already).

- If you see an accident or a stranded motorist and you are alone, it is probably more helpful to call 911 on your cell phone than to stop.
- Hitchhiking is never safe.
- Neither is picking up hitchhikers. Do not allow strangers into your car.
- Do not allow strangers into your home.
- Avoid letting strangers know when you are home alone.
- Never go outside to investigate a strange noise (we've all seen that movie).
- Always let someone know where you are going, what you are doing, who you'll be with and when you will be back — especially for trips, parties, first dates, and similar situations. This is especially important when meeting an online date for the first time.
- When first getting to know someone, keep your dates in public places, such as restaurants, malls, theaters.
- Group dates are also great when you first start getting to know someone.
- Travel in groups as often as possible, especially when going to parties or clubs.
- Contract with friends to stay (and leave) together.
- Don't break those contracts.
- Understand your limitations around substances, and realize how much they can increase your risk of having something bad happen.
- Do not leave food or drink unattended in public places, especially in bars.

Know that at some point in your life, it's likely that someone will try to seriously harm you in some way; remember that most people who are sexually victimized know their rapists,[1] and understand that if you have poor instincts or boundaries, you can be easily manipulated.

This is what to do if you are attacked:
- If you are mugged, throw your wallet, bag, or valuable items away from you — the attacker is probably more interested in those than in you. Carrying a fake wallet is a great idea.
- When you can, run.
- When you can run, run loudly!
- If you are attacked and there is no safe alternative (like running), then decide to defend yourself and do it immediately.
- Take the fight to them. Cut off their attack and incapacitate them. Do this loudly.
- The elbow is the strongest point in your body. If you are close enough to use it, use it.
- Go for the squishy parts: eyes and balls. Try to take out their vision and/or wind.
- Strike with total disregard for their safety.
- Never regret anything you do to save your own life. Self-defense classes are a really good idea for everyone.

☛ *A special note about date-rape drugs:* Date-rape drugs are chemicals that can be put into your drink that weaken you and impair your ability to move or remember things.

There are three main kinds of date-rape drugs:
  • gamma-hydroxybutyrate (GHB)
  • Rohypnol, also called rophys (pronounced "roofies")
  • ketamine hydrochloride[2]

These drugs are typically colorless and odorless, and can be easily slipped into drinks, such as soda or alcohol, without being detected. Do not accept drinks that are handed to you by someone you don't know well (unless you watched it being made). Don't leave your drink unattended. If you must leave it, leave it with a trusted friend (emphasis on *trusted*), or get a new one when you come back. Be aware of your surroundings and trust your gut.

If you taste or see anything strange in your drink, or begin to feel strange:
  • Stop drinking immediately.
  • Let someone nearby know what you suspect has happened (these chemicals can begin working very quickly).
  • Ask them to call the police.

At some point, someone may offer you one of these for recreational use or because "it's fun" or "makes sex better." Don't do it. These are sedative and hypnotic drugs that are used during medical procedures, not recreational drugs.

☛ *A special note about victims:* Victimization can cause feelings of anger, fear, guilt, and shame, and thoughts of resentment and revenge. How you handle these thoughts and feelings is very important.

When something we have no control over is done to us, we are victimized. But we have control over whether we think of ourselves as a victim. Many victims blame themselves for other people's physical and emotional violence; create or perpetuate situations that re-create pain, drama, and trauma; or take on characteristics of their perpetrators. Victims can also push away people who care, focus of what has happened in the past, and fail to take responsibility for moving forward into the future.

This is easy to do.

But it's possible to shift from that victim stance, or mentality, to a more powerful stance, by moving away from victim characteristics (passivity toward others;

harmful, overindulgent behaviors toward ourselves, or by becoming an aggressor ourselves) with actions such as active coping, personal power, and surrounding ourselves with supportive and caring people. In this way, we can move from being a victim to being someone who has been victimized.

This is *not* easy to do.

Therapy can help identify and avoid destructive thoughts and patterns, such as bottling up feelings, painting them onto other people, behaving in risky or dangerous ways, and using substances. Therapy can also help victims find creative and constructive ways, such as expression, activism, and even forgiveness, to deal with the negative thoughts and feelings.

Emotional and mental pain, like physical pain, can eventually ease. Things may not always be the same as they were before, but through coping and adjusting, our experiences, our futures, and our selves can be redefined.

Anyone can be victimized. That doesn't mean they have to be a victim.

PART FIVE
ONLINE SAFETY

CHAPTER 20
Exposure and Exploitation

Some websites are cool, others are lame, and some contain so-called "adult" content. Some are demeaning, racist, sexist, hateful, violent, or contain false information. Many sites contain material that can be disturbing, even for adults. You cannot "un-see" things, so it is very important to choose your websites and media carefully.

The Internet is a tool, and, though it can be entertaining, it should be taken very seriously. Like a weapon or a car, if you don't know what you are doing, or screw around too much, really bad things can happen. Generally, it is a good idea to avoid sites that make you uncomfortable. It is always possible to pause, stop, and delete anything you need to — even if you have already begun downloading or viewing it.

Avoid areas of the Internet that
- focus on negative, inappropriate, or unsafe sex;
- promote hate speech, bigotry, and other forms of prejudice;
- revolve around violence and offensive behavior, especially the oppression of or violence toward others based on race, national origin, language, age, disability, sex, gender, or orientation.

When you encounter these things, it's best to immediately leave by clicking on the "Home" icon, going to another site, or shutting down your browser.

The anonymity of screens can give financial, emotional, physical, and sexual predators easier access to prey. Websites sometimes ask for personal information. Don't ever give out the following information online:
- full name
- parents' names
- home address
- passwords
- phone number
- Social Security number
- credit card number
- school, sports, or work schedule

If someone asks you for this info, do not give it to them and tell an adult immediately.

Never give out any information about yourself, or your friends or family without first checking with them. Some websites ask your permission to download a program or "plug in." In some cases, these programs can be used to display unwanted advertising on your computer, but they can also invade your privacy by tracking what you're doing online, planting viruses, and increasing your risk of being hacked. Don't download anything unless you're certain it is from a trustworthy source.

Not everything that is free online is actually free. There are consequences to both providing and downloading pirated and copyrighted materials. You need to understand that the motives for people who rip off and share are not always altruistic. Part of growing up means choosing not to steal from artists — particularly those you say you admire.

Pay particular attention to people trying to start conversations in messages, chat rooms, or while gaming about something other than the topic for which the chat room was designed. Be especially cautious when someone attempts to turn a conversation sexual when there is nothing sexual about the site.

Avoid people who refuse to hear "no" or who ignore your attempts to change the subject — those are go-to tactics for online predators. Do not make physical contact with anyone you meet online without the permission of your parents. (The same goes for telephone contact.)

If you do decide to meet someone you only know online, make sure you
- meet in a public place;
- verify their identification ahead of time, including a phone number they answer, or find their name and picture on a social networking site;
- give a parent or friend that information, or take someone with you.

🐂 *Another special note about online dating:* Online dating is a great way to meet interesting people, although it can also put you in potentially vulnerable situations with people you know nothing about, with no connection to coworkers, friends, or family.

Some people snap a picture of their date when they do meet, and text it to a friend (selfie-style) as a security measure. Anyone you choose to date who is mature, responsible, and cares about women (in their life as well as in the larger community) will *not* be annoyed or offended by this. If they are put out or give you any level of crap for being appropriately cautious for your own safety, then don't let them date you.

Exploitation

According to the Crimes Against Children Research Center, one out of five U.S. teenagers who are active online have received an unwanted sexual solicitation via the Internet. These solicitations were sexual talk, requests to engage in sexual activities, or requests for personal information.

One-third of American teens have received an aggressive sexual solicitation in the past year. This means a predator has
- asked a young person to meet somewhere,
- called a young person on the phone,
- sent correspondence, money, or gifts through the U.S. Postal Service.

Behaviors like these are called grooming. Grooming is a way that child molesters and other predators try to make people vulnerable, to drop their guard or get them to trust them. It can be hard to notice when people with bad intentions are trying to groom you, because grooming often feels good. Predators will give compliments, time, keep secrets, even give money, but in the end they will ask you to do something that is not smart, not safe, and probably sexual. Grooming is a flavor of manipulation, and groomed people often feel they owe the other person or are in some other way obligated to trust them or do what they say.

Seventy-seven percent of the targets for online predators are fourteen and older; 22 percent are ages ten to thirteen.[1]

The U.S. Department of Justice maintains that, on average, there is one child molester per square mile in the United States.[2] Given isolated areas such as Kansas or the Appalachians and the vastness of places such as Texas and Alaska, this may not seem like such a big deal. However, if you acknowledge that the Internet transforms your computer screen into an open window between your home and virtually anyplace else in the world, these stats take on new meanings. Online gaming, social networking, and certain apps can make this job easier for predators.

The Breck Foundation (*breckbednar.com*) is a great resource for online safety and raising awareness about online grooming by predators.

Report sexual exploitation, harassment, grooming, abuse, and threats to
- your parents
- your Internet service provider
- the CyberTipline online (*cybertipline.com*) or 1-800-843-5678
- your local police

☛ *A special note about human trafficking:* Human trafficking is when someone forces someone else to do labor and/or sexual things in order to make money, such as forced prostitution, selling a kidnapped person as a "sex slave," or making someone pose for pornographic pictures. This kind of slavery happens all over the world. In fact, it is the third-largest international crime industry (right behind drugs and weapons trafficking).[3]

There are approximately 10 million to 30 million slaves in the world today.[4] People of every race, age, religion, and gender can be trafficked, controlled, and forced to work or made to participate in the sex trade, though most of the human trafficking victims in the world are female and younger than 18.

Sex traffickers (often called "pimps") manipulate both girls and boys (although mostly girls) in person and online (mostly online) with promises of things like love, protection, escape, and adventure.

The average age of trafficked girls is about 12 to 14 years old (boys are targeted a bit younger, at 11 to 13 years old).[5] Some victims are targeted online and tricked into meeting someone pretending to be someone they are not; some are kidnapped forcefully; and some are even recruited by friends or classmates who have already been trafficked — many pimps use teen girls or boys to recruit other teens.

Running away, being physically or sexually abused, having limited education or family support, and not being smart or safe online put teens at higher risk to be trafficked.

To lower the risk of you or other people you know being trafficked:
- Don't date guys who are out of high school and/or more than two years older than you (see page 102) — especially if you do not know them well, only know them online, or if they are going above and beyond their job description. It might feel like a compliment, but the older guy who wants to date a girl in high school is either not mature enough to hang with women his own age, or is purposely seeking out younger girls for some other, probably creepy reason. Think: Once you are out of high school, are you planning to go back to high school to get dates?
- Date people your own age, and always make sure they are willing to meet your friends and family.
- Always trust your gut. Older guys (or even women) who want you to model for pictures or be a client in their talent agency should always raise red flags. If something seems weird or too good to be true, it probably is.
- Trust your friends' guts. If other girls are giving you negative feedback about a

relationship or situation, you should pay attention.

- Participate in activities that you enjoy and are good at. Confidence makes you less of a target.
- Don't share personal information on the Internet.
- Don't accept social media requests from unknown people. (Yes, even if they're hot.)
- Friend and follow your parents for safety reasons (and because you're a big girl).
- Never share naked photos of yourself with your devices.
- Stop using the word "pimp" as a good thing. Pimps are criminals. They are violent; they abuse, control, and exploit people; and they steal money and lives that aren't theirs. It's not a compliment.
- Educate yourself about the issue of human trafficking at sites such as Polaris (*polarisproject.org*) and National Human Trafficking Resource Center (*traffickingresourcecenter.org*).
- Encourage your friends to do the same.
- Share your knowledge through links and posts on social media, and maybe even host an awareness event in your school or community.
- Say something if you see someone or something suspicious.
- In fact, save 888-373-7888 in your phone. This is the 24-hour hotline at the National Human Trafficking Resource Center. (Texting "befree" to 233733 also connects you to the NHTRC.) HumanTrafficking.org also provides information to combat trafficking through prevention, prosecution, and victim protection.

If you have concerns about trafficking for yourself or someone else, tell
- a parent
- your local police
- the National Human Trafficking Resource Center: 1-888-373-7888 (or text "befree" to 233733)

CHAPTER 21
Porn

In the global village that is the World Wide Web, a plethora of information is available at our fingertips. This includes information and entertainment. Unfortunately, this also includes misinformation; racist, sexist, homophobic, and other bigoted or violent information and images; and a ton of pornography.

According to a 2007 study from the University of Alberta, as many as 90 percent of boys and 70 percent of girls have been exposed to sexually explicit content at least once by the time they enter puberty.[1] This often happens accidentally, such as while completing their homework. Not only has porn moved from being an adult-only commodity, its quantity and intensity have both had their volumes turned way up, as it has seeped into almost every area of popular American culture.

There are very few kids who will not encounter pornography at some point by the time they begin high school, some during puberty,[2] and most certainly by the time they graduate from high school. Magazines that are legally restricted to adults are still kept behind those stupid plastic dividers in convenience stores and require ID for purchase, yet obscene, graphic, high-definition images (of things that do not necessarily need to be in HD) are easily accessed online.

Several factors contribute to this, including
- the financial rewards for the producers who can make money from people's insecurities and natural inquisitiveness,
- the lack of a walled online village for young people,
- the technology available to underagers and their knowledge of how to navigate them,
- the ease of posting and downloading amateur or homemade images and text as well as the pay-to-view stuff,
- unsolicited push porn, such as pop-up ads, banners, and keyword searches that turn even innocent and legitimate pages and searches into pathways to pornography exposure.

☛ ***One more note about pornography:*** Porn, in particular, has a much different meaning than it did just a generation ago. Pornography used to be relatively hard to come by. In the '80s, the average age of first exposure to pornography was sixteen. The average age of pornography exposure today is estimated to be eleven.[3] Young people today actually have to expend more energy to *avoid* pornography than their parents ever spent trying to get their hands on the stuff!

Porn can be particularly problematic for people who
- have not yet developed the ability (or even the motivation) to navigate relationships,
- have not had any education around sex or safety,
- are still impressionable and have yet to solidify their self-concepts,
- have bodies (as well as brains) that have not yet fully developed.

Porn objectifies women. It reduces them to parts and things, puts the first and primary focus on genitals, and eliminates any perceived need to connect with a partner emotionally or intellectually (which tends to be very important for women).

Porn objectifies men, too, fueling a whole new generation of guys with body shame and self-esteem issues, and creating anxiety for those who don't happen to want a large amount of or highly varied sexual activity at any given moment.

Porn can create and perpetuate social awkwardness and intimacy anxiety. By the age of twenty-two, the average guy has played 10,000 hours of video games[4] (mostly in isolation) and has watched (at least parts of) fifty porn videos a week[5] (again, mostly in isolation). Boys who become obsessed with Internet porn are training their brains to need a kind of stimulation that is unobtainable from a real human being.

Porn can morph expectations around types and amounts of sex, stressing performance and conquest. It also deemphasizes safety measures and pacing, essentially hard-wiring a template that is only focused on the man's timing and needs.

Make sure that you do not let it warp your values, your self-esteem, or your sense of self as a sexual person.

Choose your sites carefully. You cannot "un-see" things.

Be aware of how porn can have an impact on your expectations about sex, sexuality, and relationships. Girls can tell if a guy learned how to "do sex" by watching porn. They do not consider it a good thing.

If you choose to consume porn, don't let it take up more than 50 percent of the time you masturbate. For the other 50 percent, masturbate using only your brain and imagination. Relying only on screens means you use zero imagination while jilling off. Imagination is crucial for flirting, dating, and maintaining things such as empathy and romance in real relationships.

Feminist porn tends to focus on acts that give women (not just men) pleasure. This genre tends to have higher production value and plot than standard, boy-centric porn. Being choosey about the porn you watch can help you be ethical, more aware of the ages and working conditions of actors, and avoid viruses and other questionable content.

You are watching too much porn if you are
- watching porn every single, bloody day;
- choosing porn instead of spending time with people;
- having problems in your life because of porn, such as getting into trouble at home, school or work, overspending, getting computer viruses, or upsetting people you care about;
- can't or won't stop even after those consequences;
- are looking at more porn than you used to have to;
- are looking at things in porn that would be illegal in real life (like anything involving animals or little kids);
- are "porn-ifying" your day-to-day life — thinking about what he would look like naked, or if she would do that thing from that video — or if you find yourself sexualizing fantasy and animated characters;
- not liking yourself because you don't date porn stars, you still have all of your pubic hair, or your breasts aren't as big as that actress';
- feeling rejected, inadequate, and unable to compete;
- feeling guilty for telling your partners they are being too rough, demanding, or rude during sex;
- having trouble getting aroused or wet unless you are viewing images.

The reward circuit in your brain becomes excited by novelty and new stuff. But your brain can also get bored after too much repeated exposure to things like video games or porn, and need more and more stimulation to get the same level of excitement that it used to.

It can also cause you to feel what are called "withdrawal symptoms"[6] (such as crankiness, anxiety, and depression) for a while when you stop playing with the games (or yourself). This is not true addiction, but it is dependence, with symptoms that can mimic attention, depression, and obsessive-compulsive disorders.

Social networking allows us to connect with others to share, grow, learn, and be exposed to things that we might never experience if left only to our "real lives." But just as in real life, it comes with its own set of rules and ways to behave (which are not that different than real life, BTW).

☛ *A special note about balance:* Online interaction is meant to pass the time, not fill it. Connecting with someone online is not the same as connecting in real life, and it is important to make sure you balance your screen time with real, human interaction and physical activities.

The American Academy of Pediatrics advocates that you spend no more than an hour or two per day engaged in entertainment media. That works out to ten to fifteen hours a week.[1] If you are using online entertainment for more hours a week than you are doing your homework or hanging out with friends, it can lead to attention issues, sleep and school problems, weight gain, and wrecking your real-life strategies and skills for getting friends and dates. Do not allow online social networking to be the primary focus of your day, time, or energy.

Here is a simple exercise to help you see how balanced your life is. Chart how much time (in hours) you spend per day on the following activities for one week.

	Activity	Hours/day
1	Chores	
2	Exercise	
3	Job/work	
4	Relationships	
5	Screens	
6	School/homework	
7	Sleep	

If row number five totals more than rows one through four combined, you're out of balance. If row five is more than half of either row six or row seven, you're out of balance. Successful people exercise their brains in multiple ways, with activities such as reading, art, sports, hobbies, and conversation with other humans.

☞ *A special note about "like culture":*
Since you were babies, you've been having relationships and making connections better than the boys. It's one of your girl superpowers. Social media is one of many ways to do this.

As girls, you are very in tune to relationships, but sometimes (because girls tend to do this differently than boys) you are socialized to be more aware of how others perceive you and are more encouraged to try to be "liked" by all.

We all like receiving attention by way of likes, comments, retweets, and upvotes on social media. It can light up the brain's reward centers and trigger a hit of dopamine that feels good to everyone, and can feel very addictive for others.

It is imperative that you make sure you have other, real-world ways to get your self-esteem needs met that do not involve screens.

FOMO is an acronym for the Fear of Missing Out; that creepy feeling we sometimes get when we are not plugged into our devices and we sense that "something cool or important is happening somewhere and I am missing it!"

Social media is meant to pass the time, not fill it. It is meant to help communicate with others, but not for truly connecting. It's important to create space in our lives to unplug, but if you find that you are having a hard time doing that without having a FOMO reaction, then that is definitely something you need to work on.

A similar phenomenon called **"Facebook depression"** occurs when comparing yourselves to others' cool blogs or profiles, friends and followers, posts, pictures, bodies, lives and likes leaves you feeling increasingly crappy about yourself.

As a woman, you are way more susceptible to this kind of depression than men. Remember that most people are more likely to post about the exciting, fun, funny, and positive things that are happening, not the sucky parts of their lives. Everyone has pain, and it's important to remember we are not alone.

The following guidelines can help you protect your reputation, your loved ones, and yourself as you interact through your screens:

No one is ever as anonymous as they think they are, and what you post today can come back to haunt you later. The Internet is forever.

• Use privacy settings and options for limiting messages, and manage your updates and audiences to increase your freedom around being your authentic self online.

- Set regular dates to review and update your privacy policies.
- Do not speak negatively on your feed about friends, enemies, exes, parents, teachers, or bosses.
- Avoid constant negativity, cussing, oversharing, spoiling, poor grammar, and misspellings.
- Remember that, much like a tattoo, the nudity, grotesque or funny jokes, *Jackass*-style antics, or explicit song lyrics you post today will still be associated with you in the future.
- Remember that your future in-laws, employers, college registrars, and grandchildren will likely be able to see your posts.
- Check the facts of your updates before posting so you don't look like an idiot. (*Snopes.com* is your friend.)
- Friend and follow only people you want to be associated with. Don't be shy about unfriending people you no longer feel comfortable being connected to or associated with.
- Likewise, don't be shy about untagging yourself from photos or asking others to remove photos of you from their pages if such posts jeopardize your comfort, relationships, or reputation.
- Do not tag others in photos or posts without permission, especially if it includes risky or embarrassing behavior.
- When other people express hate and complain, strive to ignore rather than engage with them.
- Do not waste time or energy trying to correct those people who use social networking to spread hate or lies.
- Do not post when rushing, exhausted, drunk, high, or really, really pissed off.

Remember that social networking accompanies real-world interaction, and that it does not replace it.

- Balance your online life with real, warm human contact; socially responsible, and age-appropriate activities, relationships, and physical exercise.
- Realize that friending online is not the same as real life, and that the number of friends you have online is not a real-world badge of how cool, popular, interesting, or hot you are.
- Unplug from technology when in the company of family, friends, colleagues, and clients.
- Don't allow social networking to replace the "realness" of face-to-face communication.
- Remember that it's social media, not your diary or therapist.

- Don't make it easier for strangers to connect with you more than your own loved ones.

Understand that to err is human, but to seriously aggravate a situation requires an Internet connection.

- Do not share passwords with anyone except your parents.
- Be respectful of the rules and always follow the terms of use for the social platform you are using.
- Spellcheck is your friend.
- While you're at it, actually spell out words.
- Do not post anything you wouldn't say in a face-to-face interaction.
- Actual human beings read the words you post, text, or send, so remember, your computer does not give you free rein to be cruel or rude.
- Have a litmus test for whom you friend or follow. For example, only people you would invite to your house for dinner or buy a birthday gift for.

Understand that while you are online, manners still matter. Tweet others the way you want to be tweeted.

- Remember that kindergarten rules such as saying "please" and "thank you" still apply.
- Show patience and kindness to newbies.
- Do your legitimate best to not offend anyone with your content.
- Do not tweet or post from the bathroom.
- Ever.
- Be mindful about what personal information you share, but use your real picture, real name, and real age in your profile.
- Choose a picture that reflects how you would like to be perceived by your friends, family, and associates.
- Don't spoil it when you live-tweet sporting events, award ceremonies, elections, or season finales. Post spoiler alerts, so people can take a break from your feed for the night. Otherwise, wait a day or two before posting specific spoilers.
- Speaking of spoiling, do not "vulture" other people's posts by posting about others getting married, pregnant, or raises; moving; breaking up; or coming out until they post it first.
- Do not call out, humiliate, or gossip about people online — it's social networking, not reality television.
- Do not poach others' friend lists just because you think someone is hot. Ask for an introduction first.

- When you send friend requests to people you do not know well, attach a message with an introduction.
- Beware of oversharing and avoid topics such as bodily functions, anything involving bodily fluids, and personal hygiene mishaps.
- Balance your feeds with philosophical and funny, positive and negative, the silly and the cerebral.
- Give love by being charitable with other people's observations and content, and don't just talk about yourself.

☛ *A special note about apps:* There are loads of apps out there that encourage sneaky, inappropriate, and sometimes illegal behavior. It is important, in the service of being a responsible person, to not spend your time, energy, or money investing in apps that
- mask your identity,
- promote cruel behavior,
- encourage you to lie,
- help you break the law,
- make it easy to be located by people you do not know.

Using those apps gives your time, energy, and money to developers who encourage irresponsible behavior, take advantage of stupid people, and support the predators who prey on them.

If you have to lie about your online behavior, you are not in control of your life.

CHAPTER 23
Sexting

Flirting and impulsive choices are in the job description of anyone with "teen" in their age. It has been that way forever, but it is important to understand the major difference between past, current, and future generations: Now, everyone has a camera with them at all times.

Everyone has done things that are stupid, impulsive, uncharacteristic, or possibly even illegal, and most of the time, these are done during adolescence and get worked out of your system. However, now we all have technology at a pocket's reach to document these things and share them with our friends, and their friends, and their friends, which means it doesn't get "worked out of our system" anymore — it gets advertised.

Sending graphic images and pornographic videos via text message to friends is becoming such a problem that major cities have entire teams on their police forces dedicated to sexting and Internet crimes. This trend of sending sexual texts and pictures via cell phones has led to a number of teens being charged with child pornography.[1]

☛ *A special note about child pornography:* Any naked image of anyone younger than 18 can be defined as child pornography, even if it is their own naughty bits.

- It is a felony to create child pornography.
- It is a felony to distribute child pornography over media lines.
- It is a felony to possess child pornography.

Felony. Felony. Felony.

Under federal law, child pornography is a criminal act, and is defined as any kind of drawing, cartoon, sculpture, painting, photograph, film, video, computer-generated image, or picture that depicts a minor engaging in obscene, sexually explicit conduct.[2] These illegal images can be produced and presented in various forms, including print media, videotape, film, CD, the Internet, and yes, cell phones, and teens found distributing or possessing such images can be found guilty of child pornography.

It is only called "sexting" when *everyone* involved is older than 18. Otherwise, it's child pornography.

It is also important to remember that, although sexting — I mean child pornography — is generally exchanged between friends, it does not always stay that way. Once something is sent over the Internet, you lose all control over what happens to it. Any picture or text you create, send, or pass on could exist (and be traced back to you) in perpetuity (that means forever). Remember, the Internet is forever.

If you are a teen girl and are reading this book, chances are you have had a guy ping you a picture of his penis that you did not ask to see.

Testosterone is a good thing. It helps both create and conquer challenges, and it contributes to creativity, drive, and stamina in both men and women. Unfortunately, it also raises libido and risk taking, making some people — particularly boys — sometimes look like maniacs.

You do not have to put up with that.

Pop quiz: If a guy pulled his penis out and showed it to you in a parking garage, what would you do?

    A) Point and laugh.
    B) Call the police.
    C) Just put up with it.
    D) Tell him to knock it off.
    E) Tell a grown-up to tell him to knock it off.

There is no wrong answer. Well, except for C. C is a wrong answer. Whatever action you choose to take, it should be no different when such behavior happens on your phone.

The problem is, a lot of guys now think this is flirting. In case some of you have also fallen into this trap: It. Is. Not. Flirting.

Whatever you do, do not respond positively. When they send those pictures to you and you think *Eww, gross/he likes me!* and then send a pic back, he thinks, "Score! It worked!" creating a negative, pornified cycle. Do not encourage that behavior. One-third of girls (statistically) have sent a nude selfie to someone, and depending on which study you read, sometimes girls even start that cycle. Please don't do that, either.

I want you to understand a few things:
- Sending people pictures of your swimsuit areas will definitely get you attention.
- But those areas are going get attention even when they are covered by a sweater or jeans.

- Boys do not think of those pictures as a special, intimate favor or a grand gesture of trust that builds your relationship and brings the two of you closer. When you send them a picture, they just think: "Boobs!" Period.
- When you choose to not send them pictures, they will just get them from someone else. Or they will Google them. (They're going to do that, anyway.)
- The sense of self-worth and level of mystery you show when you don't give your pics out like Pokemon cards can be a lot more interesting. Refuse to be a statistic or some random, faceless picture in an album on some dude's phone.

I want to challenge each of you reading this to care enough about yourself to choose the attention you get from your suitors, male or female, on purpose. This means:

- Move at your own pace, and demand they first give attention to the beauty and fantastic things you have to offer under your skin not just under your clothes.
- Make them appreciate what's between your ears more than what's between your legs.
- Wait for them to show interest and curiosity about your heart before you let them anywhere near your chest.

Ten Big-Girl Rules for Flirting Digitally

1. Be 18!
2. Otherwise, keep it PG-13; stick to compliments, questions, comments about things that have already happened and pictures with clothes on.
3. Don't do anything in a text that you haven't done in person yet.
4. Do not make future promises.
5. If you can't talk about it, you shouldn't be doing it. If you wouldn't want your best friend, mom, or doctor to know, then stop. If you wouldn't say it to their faces, then don't text it.
6. Reserve those special pictures for people with whom you have been together long enough to have made it past a good fight (or two).
7. And/or you've met each other's significant friends and/or family.
8. And/or you've survived some sort of dramatic or traumatic situation together, such as the death of a pet, a road trip, or a work crisis.
9. Again, be 18!
10. Listen to your gut and trust your instincts. If something tells you it is not the right time or the right person, do not hit "send."

Oh yeah, and when you come across one of those maniacs who is irresponsible with pictures, personal information, reputation, or heart? Tell everyone. (Networking is one of your girl superpowers.)

CHAPTER 24

Cyberbullying

Cyberbullying is when someone embarrasses, harasses, threatens, or attacks someone else by using technology, such as phones, computers, and tablets, as well as social media sites, text messages, chat, apps, and websites.

Examples of cyberbullying include
- forwarding personal or private messages or pictures;
- posting pictures without consent;
- writing mean, scary, or violent text messages, posts, or emails;
- spreading rumors or lies by email, text, or social media posts;
- posting embarrassing pictures, videos, or memes;
- using fake pages, memes, or profiles;
- using modifying software to publicly embarrass someone with fake pictures or memes;
- catfishing/tricking other people online into saying or doing things that are vulnerable or embarrassing;
- making direct threats or personal attacks;
- "subtweeting" — spreading rumors, lies, or mean comments on any platform (not just Twitter) about someone without naming them directly, but using enough information so that everyone (usually including the victim) knows who is being discussed. It still counts as cyberbullying.

Mean comments and damaging rumors are the most common types of cyberbullying. Revenge, justice, and, "just 'cuz" are the most common reasons given for it. Social networking sites and texts are the most common vehicles.

The psychological and emotional effects of cyberbullying are similar to those of real-life bullying, but can be much more damaging.

- In real life, bullying often ends when the school day ends, but cyberbullying can happen 24 hours a day, seven days a week. This means that people can still be bullied and humiliated even in their own homes.
- Mean and embarrassing information can be posted anonymously and distributed quickly to a very wide audience. This embarrassment feels large and public, and it often is.
- Deleting, stopping, or refuting the harassment or rumors is extremely difficult after the messages, texts, or pictures have been posted or sent.
- Unlike bullying that occurs in person, there are not usually teachers or other

adults available to offer intervention, protection, or help and support, so victims often are left feeling very alone.

Things to understand about cyberbullying

The anonymity that screens enable is very tempting, even for adults — just look at the comment threads underneath any given online article. Everyone who interacts with other humans on the Internet witnesses cruel behavior sooner or later. It happens to all of us.

It happens by accident, too. Just because you feel hurt, humiliated, and harassed does not necessarily mean the other person intended it. Online interactions don't allow for eye contact, body language, voice inflection, and a bunch of other things that are involved in real communication.

If you know the person who just hurt your feelings, if you trust the person who just did something that seemed rude, if you heard that person was the source of your humiliation but you have considered that person a friend ... check it out face to face.

Boys tend to be more aggressive when they bully each other; girls can do more damage to each other through more passive or subtler ways, such as relational bullying.

Relational bullying can look like this:
- spreading rumors or gossip from the bully,
- sending or forwarding messages for or from the bully,
- encouraging the bully by laughing or liking their behavior or posts,
- standing by and saying or doing nothing.

Sharing stuff or dropping random comments when we're not face to face with someone can hurt just as much as (if not more than) active bullying. If you hurt someone in an online interaction, apologize and make it right.

☛ *A special note about constructive criticism:* The examples of what not to do are much louder and shinier than the examples of how to do it right. Unfortunately, there is not a lot of role modeling about giving constructive criticism.

Criticism focuses only on what you don't like. That is super unhelpful, wastes time and energy, and changes nothing unless you also focus on being constructive. This means that you are bothering to take time out of your life to offer an opinion because
- the topic actually matters to you,

- you want something else, different, or better to happen.

Commenting just because you hate something is childish, often misdirected, and most people only do it to feel powerful and blow off their own steam. It's like yelling at a waiter because you didn't like your steak.

So, in service of not bullying others when commenting online, here is a checklist of how to give helpful and constructive criticism:
  - Ask yourself if this thing or issue is really important to you, and why.
  - Ask yourself if your opinion is going to change anyone's mind. Do not waste your time arguing with stupid or crazy people. That never ends well.
  - Keep it simple. Focus on the words and behavior. This is about the thing, not the person.
  - Start off with "I" (like "I think the thing … " or "I believe the issue … ") not "you."
  - Identify what it is you do not like or disagree with.
  - Explain why (please do your homework before you go spouting off).
  - Deliver your response in a factual, mature, polite way.
  - Don't engage with people who only comment randomly about things or people they do not actually give a crap about, or who are hateful and just doing it to make themselves feel better (rather than to improve the situation).

Kids are mean to each other and always have been, but the viciousness and the viral aspects of doing it remotely, online, are prolific. Bullying occurs in every school, and even if you haven't been a direct victim of it, we all know someone who has. Almost half of all teens say they have been bullied online.[1] Anyone can be a target.

Cyberbullying can have loads of harmful effects, such as depression, feelings of isolation, and low self-esteem. There are many other negative effects, but these particular three also happen to be three major risk factors for suicide among teens.[2] Cyberbullying can escalate extremely quickly, and the consequences can be tragic. Studies show that 10 percent of cyberbullying victims contemplate suicide — three times more than kids who are not cyberbullied.[3]

Some people don't understand that the hate they bring with their actions can have a very heavy and powerful impact on the other end, and that some people choose to end their own life because of someone else's thoughtlessness. Thoughtless and irresponsible posting can have just as powerful and as tragic an effect as intentional cyberbullying.

It is important to acknowledge the damage and harm that cyberbullying can do to those who are the victims. It is also important to understand that this kind of violence feeds on itself. Sixty-six percent of teens who have witnessed online cruelty have also witnessed others joining in.[4] Thirty-four percent of those who have had any engagement in cyberbullying have been both a cyberbully and been cyberbullied.[5]

Some kids, instead of hurting themselves, lash out and choose to become the bully and start harming others offline, as well. A study by the National Threat Assessment Center found that in more than two-thirds of school shootings, the shooters felt "persecuted, bullied, or threatened." In more than half of the shootings, revenge was the main motivation.[6]

- A powerful woman pays attention to how she and her friends are treated online.
- A powerful woman pays attention to how she and her friends treat others online.
- A powerful woman doesn't stand by and watch bullying happen to those who don't have friends to do this for them.

If you witness anyone being bullied online, do not just stand by. You can help support the victim (as well as future victims) by standing up for a friend and telling a trusted adult, such as a teacher, parent, or coach. Save the posts to show as evidence. Above all, do not fight bullies by becoming one.

Here are some things you can do in a bullying situation:
- Don't contribute to the harm or participate in ignoring or talking about other people.
- Physically leave the situation or conversation thread if you must.
- Don't become a bully by delivering someone else's message.
- If there are problems between friends, encourage the people to talk to each other.
- Ask the bully how they would feel if this happened to them.
- Stand up to friends and peers and refuse to trick, be mean to, or exclude people.
- Encourage other people to get consent before spreading someone else's business that may be personal.

What to say to someone who has (or you think might have) been bullied:
- Tell them what you heard.
- Ask if they are OK.
- Tell them it is not their fault.
- Let them know you do not agree with what happened.
- Tell them not to reciprocate.

- Encourage them to tell an adult.
- Offer to help them do that.
- Offer to do something social with them, lunch, studying, an activity after school, etc.
- Let them know you are there for them.
- Check in with them later.

What else can you do?

- Remember that bullies, at their core, are victims, too. They are not more powerful than you. That's why they are doing this so publicly — they are trying to make you *think* they are more powerful.
- Remember that by crossing the line, breaking school rules or sometimes the law by bullying you, bullies give all of their power up to you.
- Use your words, not your device. Tell someone, so the bully can be caught and punished.
- Then, use your device and block their ass.
- It is important to never, ever respond to a cyberbully; that only makes it worse. If you want to show someone you are upset, show your friends and family, who will support you. Showing the bullies you are upset will encourage them to continue targeting you.
- Do not lash out if you have been victimized. Seek help.
- If your school does not have a policy about cyberbullying, call school administrators on it, or get your parents to do it.
- Mind your friend lists and privacy settings.
- Create strong passwords, and never, ever give them out (even to your closest friend).
- Do not let someone use your phone or take your place at the computer and pretend to be you.
- Educate yourself and others about the effects of cyberbullying.
- Do not stay silent when someone else is harassed online. Report violent, sexual, and hateful behaviors to school administrators, parents, and/or police when necessary.

CHAPTER 25
Online Gaming

As online communities have grown, recreational gaming has moved online, allowing players to compete any time with like-minded players anywhere in the world. The rules of good sportsmanship and safe, responsible conduct in real-world, competitive environments (such as youth athletics, professional sports, pickup games at the park) apply to the virtual world as well.

Just as in real life, we need to remember that the kindergarten rules of sharing, taking turns, and fair play still apply.

- Be polite in your interactions online, using the same manners, language, and level of respect that you would in public.
- Familiarize yourself with the rules of each game and the terms of use for each site.
- Remember that live communication during games (whether by chat, headsets, or video) is public.
- Be a responsible player and clan teammate by communicating clearly and keeping appointments and schedules.
- Make sure your trash talk is good-natured and stays in the spirit of the site.

And, don't create sexual, violent, or offensive screen names, avatars, gamer tags, or profiles — it makes you look creepy and just invites trouble.

People who purposely try to cause trouble and harm on the Internet are referred to as "trolls." "Griefers" are a specific flavor of troll who target fellow players while gaming. They engage in aggressive behavior both in and outside the parameters of the game, such as breaking rules, unreasonable kills, threatening messages, and aggressive comments.

There are five primary tactics that trolls use:

1. **Threats and harassment.** Any game connected to the Internet allows players to contact each other through either private messages or public forums. Trolls can use these to send explicit messages or threats, or sexually harass other players.

2. **Hacking.** Trolls and bullies can hack game accounts and profiles. Once there, they can delete saved progress and items, change information, send inappropriate messages to contacts and other players, or even lock victims out of their own profile.

3. **Hate speech.** Trolls can rage at a specific person about specific things or can take their hate global and go racist, anti-Semitic, homophobic, and anti-woman. Hate speech is taken very seriously by most gaming platforms, and it violates their code of conduct or terms and conditions.

4. **Infection.** When playing online, trolls can sabotage groups or specific targets by posting links and codes that can install viruses in other users' computers or gaming systems.

5. **Doxing.** Trolls can maliciously share other people's personal and identifying information, including passwords, phone numbers, and physical addresses.

If (or when) trouble finds you, all gaming systems provide ways to ignore, stop, or block players who use inappropriate behavior or language, or cheat or attack. When other players do these things, do not reciprocate — that just increases their negative behavior.

Here are some of the most popular games' direct contacts to report abusive behavior:

Minecraft: *minecraft@minecraft.ign.com*
Xbox Live: *xbox.com/en-US/live/abuse*
Playstation Network: *us.playstation.com*
Wii Network: *nintendo.com/consumer/webform*

☛ *A special note about girls and gaming:* Playing video games has come a long way, and they are not just for those stereotypical, pale, shiny boys who smell of Red Bull and Cheetos. They have evolved, and appeal to people of all ages and genders. There are games for everyone. However, certain games (and certain aspects of gaming culture itself) lend themselves to a sometimes toxic mix of testosterone, high emotion, and the anonymity of screens.

Research supports the notion that for women, gaming is the least welcoming of all of the online environments,[1] and that women, in particular, are more likely to be targets of physical threats, sexual harassment, and stalking.

As a girl, if you play video games, the most important thing you should know is that certain types of games lend themselves to more aggressive attitudes than others do. If you play these games, accept the reality that, at some point, you will be targeted with gender-based, sexually influenced, misogynistic, and hateful messages, simply because you are a woman. In fact, you are statistically 25 times more likely to be the target of sexually explicit, threatening, and malicious messages if your screen name, user profile, or avatar is feminine.[2]

When this happens, here are some things that you (as a woman) can do:

- Tell the trolls to stop. Tell them that further action will result in authorities being contacted. Tell them this once and once only.

- Then block and report their ass. All game systems have blocking and reporting options, and sometimes (mostly because of these issues) even formal complaint processes through which the more aggressive jerks can be properly banned.

- Remember that no matter how personal a troll may try to make it, these attacks are not about you; they're about what you represent to the troll. If you take action quickly and remove that player's ability to continue to target you, the person's motivation can be diminished.

- Talk to your parent(s) and friends. Not only do you not have to put up with misogynistic crap, but you don't have to deal with it alone.

- Talk to other players on your team or in your clan. They can offer support and help you complain, report, and block as well.

- You can also contact game moderators, the website hosting the interaction, and other players' ISP providers.

- Contact the police if the troll is actually threatening things that would be illegal in real life, such as threats of death, rape, or other bodily harm (especially if you have the sense that the person on the other side of that screen is anywhere in the vicinity of serious).

- Keep evidence of any threats. Digital records may be important if any legal action is taken later, but pictures, screenshots, and time stamps are important as well.

- Do not stand by and watch these people do it to someone else. Say something, either in support of the target or about the behavior of the aggressor (but do not engage the aggressor directly). When you engage (or "feed") the trolls, it only makes their behavior worse. But by doing what you can to turn the troll's obnoxious and toxic behavior back on the troll, where it belongs, it helps everyone — including, quite possibly, the troll. When aggressors' own behavior causes them enough distress, they will be motivated to change.

Remember that networking is one of your superpowers. Re-blogging or re-posting a bully's hateful posts and messages in forums or on social media can help raise awareness — just be cautious about sharing that bully's screen name or picture. Instead, share a thoughtful message about being a good digital citizen, the dangers of cyberbullying, or link to information or a support page from websites such as *cybersmile.org, cyberbullying.org,* or *beheroes.net.* Doing so can turn something someone originally meant for harm into something that could potentially help someone else or raise awareness.

The Internet is a place as much as it is a thing, and bad guys always go where kids are. The anonymity and interactive features of games make them a favorite destination of more than half a million online predators every day.[3] They use games to get to kids, because when you are distracted and focusing on the game, you are easier to manipulate. It's the same reason that pickpockets hang out in crowded streets, except that what these guys want from inside your pants is not your wallet.

Until you are in high school, only communicate online with people you have actually met in real life. And save video chat until you are at least sixteen. I know that sucks, but it really is one of the best ways to keep yourself (and your friends) safe. Now, roll your eyes back into the forward position and keep reading.

Do not give out personal information to anyone while gaming, including your full name, address, passwords, phone number, or Social Security or credit card numbers (or anyone else's). Choose not to fall for people trying to get personal information from you by giving you compliments, gifts, tips, or points. Beware of others trying to start conversations over chat about something other than the game, and be especially cautious when someone attempts to turn a conversation sexual. This will happen at some point.

A very popular tactic that bad guys use is to pretend to be someone your age, spend some time chatting you up, and eventually ask to see you without your clothes on. When this happens, try this test: Refuse and change the subject. If the person soliciting you is actually a kid, too, they will back off. If they keep pushing or refuse to hear "no," it's a sign that they are either a creepy adult trying to get a pic of you naked or they are another kid with really bad boundaries and judgment.

Even if they send you a pic of what they claim to be themselves naked, it could be a lie; it may be a picture of the last kid they duped into sending them a selfie. If you do find yourself super tempted to send a pic to anyone, see "A special note about child pornography" (page 130).

Never, ever make physical contact with anyone you have met online without the permission of your parents and someone to accompany you. While you are at it, be a good digital citizen: If you see that someone else is not following these basic safety guidelines, or is being pressure by other people not to, say something. You'd get that person's back if someone was trying to flank or snipe them in the game, right?

Another important thing to remember with online gaming is that it is online. This means that the same safety guidelines of the Internet apply here as well (see page 126). Protect yourself with strong passwords (the more characters the better) that include a mix of letters, numbers, and symbols, and don't share them with anyone except your family. Talk to your folks when you see or hear things during gaming that bother, upset, or gross you out. Know how (and be willing to) report inappropriate violent, sexual, and hate behaviors to game administrators, your parents, and/or police when necessary. This is especially important when someone pressures you for personal information, sends you disturbing materials, or asks to meet you in real life.

Other thoughts about gaming responsibly:
- Make media and gaming a family activity whenever possible.
- Balance out your games (platform, adventure, shooter, RPG, strategy, sports, simulation) and try not to focus on only one genre or flavor.
- Unplug on occasion and play games that involve cards, boards, pawns, and dice — not just screens.
- Treat gaming as a privilege and a reward for hard work and achieved goals (such as completed homework and chores).
- Keep in mind that "mods" (user-generated, downloadable pieces of content meant to be added to a game) are not rated by the Entertainment Software Rating Board (ESRB)*, that the games' designers are not responsible for their content, and that they may contain violent, sexual, or offensive content.
- Only download content from reliable sources, not random links or unverified sites, because they may contain offensive material, malware, or other kinds of spam.
- Choose not to steal from developers and companies you respect and admire.
- Do not play pirated or unlicensed copies of games, and encourage your friends to do the same.
- Pay attention to ESRB guidelines and avoid age-inappropriate games.

*The ESRB independently applies ratings suggested by the industry, and suggests appropriate ages and partial lists of content in games.[4]

ESRB ratings

EC: Early childhood (ages three and older). It would be hard to find something offensive or inappropriate with these games, which generally feature music, shapes, and characters you'd recognize from television.

E: Everyone (ages six and older). These games include minimal fantasy and slapstick violence.

E10+: Everyone ages ten and older. Game possibilities include mild language, body humor, and comic mischief.

T: Teen. These games are appropriate for teens and may include more suggestive themes, cruder humor, the possibilities of blood, and stronger language.

M: Mature (ages seventeen and older). There will be violence, active gore, sexual references, and the possibilities of nudity and strong language.

AO: Adults only (ages eighteen and older). These games involve intense violence and graphic sexuality. Gambling with real-world currency would fall into this category as well.

When you have been threatened or abused while gaming, these are the order in which you should use your resources:
- your parents
- the game's hosts/moderators
- your local police
- the CyberTipline online (*cybertipline.com*) or 1-800-843-5678

The Internet Crime Complaint Center (IC3) is a partnership between the FBI, the National White Collar Crime Center and the Bureau of Justice Assistance, and they deal with more serious cases of online harassment.

PART SIX
FOR PARENTS

CHAPTER 26
The Statistical Reality

The focus of abstinence-only education is primarily on encouraging kids to say no, but that is not consistent with adolescent biology, and teens today are just as likely not to say no as they were in the past.

Research from four cycles of the National Survey of Family Growth (which studies information on sexual and marital behaviors) finds that almost all Americans have sex before marrying. According to nonmarital-sex research, this behavior is the norm in the U.S., and has been for the past fifty years.[1] A recent study published in *Public Health Reports* shows that by age twenty, 75 percent of Americans have had nonmarital sex. That number rises to 95 percent by age forty-four.[2]

Teens do not refrain from sex, even if they are scared, don't know how to protect themselves, or have been given unhelpful, negative, or shaming information.

The problem is not teens having sex. The problem is teens
  • having unprotected sex,
  • having unsafe sex,
  • becoming pregnant,
  • contracting sexually transmitted infections.

With the $1.5 billion that has been spent thus far on abstinence-only education,[3] we have learned that, at best, abstinence-only education delays the onset of sexual activity by approximately six months.[4]

We have also learned that when those same kids do start to engage in nonmarital sex (as 95 percent of Americans do), they are less likely to use protection and more likely to get pregnant than teens who have had more comprehensive sex ed.

  • An estimated 750,000 teen girls are expected to become pregnant in the next year.
  • Approximately 350,000 of these girls are between the ages of fifteen and seventeen.

- Half of these pregnancies occur within six months of becoming sexually active.
- More than 80 percent of teen pregnancies are unintended.[5]

In the U.S., three or four girls out of 10 become pregnant before they reach the age of twenty. In Europe, where they start having sex at the same time and at the same rate as in the U.S. but talk about it in school, post condom ads on billboards, and provide medically accurate information in magazines for kids and teens, the pregnancy rate is closer to six out of 100.[6]

The most common reasons American teens do not use contraception are that they
- are not planning for sex,
- don't believe pregnancy will occur,
- don't want to use birth control,
- don't know where to get birth control or protection,
- don't know how to practice safer sex,
- are not comfortable asking questions about sex in general.

Each of these ideas is easily addressed with clear and open, factual, accurate, reality-based comprehensive sexual education. Combating the rate of teen sex does not make sense. The focus should be on avoiding negative consequences.

With regard to sexuality, many adolescents
- have never discussed sex or sexuality with a supportive adult to whom they can ask questions;
- have more sex than they have knowledge;
- do not understand the difference between sex that is healthy and safer, and sex that is not;
- have sex experiences long before they are mentally, emotionally, and physically ready;
- engage in sexual behavior to satisfy nonsexual needs (such as control of a relationship, acceptance by others, or increasing their self-esteem).

Educational interventions are needed that will provide the skills and information underagers need to protect themselves from unintended pregnancy and sexually transmitted infection when they do become sexually active, regardless of their age or marital status.

Accepting these realities and giving teens the tools they need to stay safe make for a much more effective policy than giving kids information that is misleading, inaccurate, or based on our hopes for their behavior.

These kids trust us, as they should, and as we want them to. Tweens and teens need to be given opportunities to use their judgment, exercise critical-thinking muscles, and make mistakes. Because mistakes will be made — we're talking about teenagers. It is our job as the adults to be there to support them, and help them figure out what went wrong and how to fix it next time.

How do responsible parents teach their kids to drive? Simply tell them not to speed? Explain how many times seatbelts don't work? Abstinence is a good idea and should be encouraged, but it conflicts with the statistical reality, and setting it as the only expectation is not serving the young people in this country.

CHAPTER 27
The 'Gay' Issue (That Impacts Straight Kids, Too)

Despite the nearly 1 million gay teenagers in the United States,[1] and the growing acceptance of gays and lesbians in American popular culture, gay and lesbian teens are particularly uninformed and alienated by sex education classes.

Most school districts in this country advocate some form of sex education, but very few include resources and education for lesbians and gays in their curriculum. In fact, the only sex that is often discussed (and which kids are encouraged to abstain from) is penis-in-vagina intercourse.

A 2008 study from the Bradley Hasbro Children's Research Center found that more than half of fifteen- to nineteen-year-olds have oral sex, and that anal sex is increasing among straight teenagers and young adults (between 1995 and 2004, the number doubled).[2]

Straight kids participate in oral and anal sex to
 • avoid pregnancy,
 • please a partner,
 • preserve their virginity.

According to the CDC, the probability of HIV acquisition by the receptive partner in unprotected oral sex with an HIV carrier is one per 10,000 acts. In vaginal sex, it is ten per 10,000 acts. In anal sex, it's fifty per 10,000 acts.[3] This means anal sex is five times more dangerous than vaginal sex, and fifty times more dangerous than oral sex.

Abstinence education emphasizes the importance of virginity and only focuses on vaginal intercourse. Studies involving sexual and reproductive health issues find that about 10 percent of American teens have engaged in anal sex.[4]

Without the opportunity to be educated about the subject, some (especially straight) teens conclude that oral and anal sex are not real sex and therefore must not have the same risks or consequences. In fact, it is often referred to without the word sex included, as in "getting oral" or "we did anal last night."

Worse still, some teens can convince themselves that anal sex between partners of the opposite sex does not carry the same risk as "gay sex," since it isn't "gay."

This mentality is a significant risk factor for HIV and other sexually transmitted infections. It is critical that we recognize that more and more young people are engaging in anal sex, so that we can open the lines of communications and help them protect their sexual health.

According to the Sexuality Information and Education Council of the United States, 37 states require HIV and sexually transmitted infection education. Nine states require that "discussion of sexual orientation be inclusive." Four states require "only negative information" about homosexuality or "homosexual acts."[5] That's right, Alabama, South Carolina, Texas, and Utah, I'm talking about you.

Non-straight kids have to navigate adolescence and puberty in isolation in order to avoid the stigma of negative stereotypes and biases they are inundated with by mainstream popular culture.

Addressing gay issues and homosexuality in sex education could help
- address the heightened health risks faced by gays and lesbians (and those kids who do "gay and lesbian things") because of misinformation and a lack of information about safer-sex practices;
- minimize the harassment of gay and lesbian students, as well as their emotional isolation, which contributes to high suicide and dropout rates among gay teens. Forty percent of gay teens — as opposed to 10 percent of straight teens — have attempted suicide at least once, according to the *American Journal of Public Health*).[6] Gay kids are four times as likely to succeed in their attempts.[7]

In addition to suicide, these kids are at increased risk for
- mental health issues
- violence at home and at school
- harassment
- substance abuse as escapism
- pregnancy and disease. Gay kids are less likely than their straight counterparts to prepare for sexual encounters.

Sex education should address the full range of behaviors that teens engage in, whether gay or straight.

CHAPTER 28
Abstinence-only Education Versus Comprehensive Sex Education

Studies consistently conclude that abstinence-only approaches do not work. These approaches tend to focus only on risks and dangers, such as pregnancy, HIV, assault, and STIs, reinforcing negative feelings about sex, which can act as barriers to reducing risk behaviors.

An April 2007 study funded by the U.S. government to evaluate its own program was conducted by the Mathematic Policy Research Inc., which routinely conducts independent studies to evaluate policies for the U.S. government.[1] The study found that

- approximately half of all high school youth reportedly engaged in sexual activity,
- one-quarter of those kids have a sexually transmitted infection (STI).

Abstinence-only education was found to have had

- no overall impact on teen sexual activity,
- no impact on the rate of unprotected sex.

Students in abstinence-only programs had similar ages of sexual debut (14.9 years old) as those of their control-group peers.

The largest difference recorded between an abstinence-only program and the control group (which had no education) involved a program called ReCapturing the Vision. It reported 48 percent of teens in its program had remained abstinent in the previous twelve months. The control group reported 43 percent.

The study found that there was some improved knowledge of STIs; however, it also found that the youths who participated in abstinence-only education programs were less likely to believe that birth control worked, and so were less likely to use a method of birth control.

University of Washington researchers found that students who had comprehensive sex education were 60 percent less likely to become pregnant than those without any sex education, and 50 percent less likely than the abstinence-only group.[2]

Comprehensive sex education means answering questions honestly, and with medical accuracy and age appropriateness, while being consistent and respectful of the participants.

Comprehensive sex education addresses
- age-appropriate information on developmental stages
- personal skills, such as relationships and self-esteem
- discussions about choices, which means that choices need to be offered, instead of offering only one option, such as abstinence only
- cultural relevance and sexual behavior by responding to and discussing what is actually happening
- diversity — keeping the language open and focusing on one's behavior, not judgments about who the person is
- sexual health, including safety practices, options, and testing
- reliable resources

Comprehensive sex education delays the onset of intercourse, improves the frequency and success of the use of safer sex practices, and does not lead to increased sexual activity.[3]

Knowledge and self-confidence are the best protection against the unfortunate consequences that sometimes accompany sexual activity. More knowledge is better than not enough knowledge. Obviously.

Therapists like me do not avoid inquiring about suicidal thoughts in depressed clients for fear of creating more suicidal thoughts, because it's been shown to have the opposite effect. Likewise, talking to teens about sex does not lead to more sex. Besides, even if more knowledge did lead to more sex, more people having safer sex is better than anyone having unsafe sex.

Teaching children about healthy sexuality while they are still open to adult influence spares us from witnessing them putting themselves at risk later in life because of a lack of knowledge.

Thoughts of our adolescent children as sexual beings may make us uncomfortable, but visions of them tumbling down flights of stairs as toddlers spurred us to have safety conversations back then. The thought of them putting themselves through car windshields motivates us to teach them how to navigate intersections and freeways when behind the wheel. If discussion about how to navigate their genitals is different, it is quite likely because of our own discomfort with the subject matter, and that's a poor reason to avoid the topic.

Teenagers are going to have sex, as they always have. This may or may not include your child, but most teens are adults physically, even though they're not mature in a social or emotional sense. Biology often trumps social and religious mores, as well as fear, logic, and even, sometimes, laws.

Children and teens need to know that the safest sex of all is no sex, and we must help young people become self-confident enough to say "no" — despite peer and social pressures. But they also have to know what "sex" is. And they need to know what "safer sex" is. Because, sooner or later, most of them do decide to become sexually active. They need to be prepared to protect themselves before they say "yes."

We can teach them how to protect themselves and get testing or treatment if they need it. We can teach them how to be true to themselves and respectful of others. The issue is not whether teens will get sex education. The issue is how and where they will gather information, and whether the information they gather will be accurate and accessible, or unreliable or exploitative.

Young people are less likely to take sexual risks if they have
- a positive view of sexuality
- information they need to take care of their sexual health
- clarity about their own values and an understanding of their families' values
- self-esteem and self-confidence
- interpersonal skills, such as assertiveness and decision-making abilities
- an understanding of the consequences and results of both their actions and their inactions
- a connection to home, family, and other caring adults in their community and school

What parents and underagers need to know about sex

- Sex is a part of one's personality — not the most interesting or most important part, but a part.
- There are differences between sex, orientation, gender, and identity.
- No one needs to feel bad, scared, ashamed, or unclean for being a sexual creature.
- There are many healthy ways to think about and engage in sexual behavior.
- There are many unhealthy ways to think about and engage in sexual behavior.
- Relationships are integral parts of healthy sexual behavior.
- Those relationships are formed in many different ways.
- The most important relationship teens will have is their relationship with themselves.
- Sexual behavior and relationships have potential risks and benefits.
- Choosing to abstain from sexual behavior is a choice.
- Choosing to engage in sexual behavior is a choice.
- It is important to take responsibility for one's sexual choices and behavior.
- It is important to make informed decisions and healthy choices.
- One needs to take responsibility for one's sexual choices and behavior.
- It is vital for teens to discuss their feelings, have their own experiences, and develop their own attitudes about sex.
- Media, social needs, and pressure can have an impact on sexual identity.
- Strive to create a positive self-image and identity in spite of these things.
- Learn how to communicate about sex with potential partners.
- It is important to know the names and definitions of sexual words, acts, and safety measures.
- Humans are the only beings capable of consciously controlling their number

of offspring.
- Know what is involved in the processes of conception, pregnancy, and birth.
- It is important to use birth control and safer-sex methods every time one engages in sexual activity.
- Know how to access and properly use birth control and safer-sex methods.
- Know how to best avoid unwanted sexual experiences and consequences.
- Realize the social, emotional, financial, and physical consequences of failing to practice safer sex, abiding by local laws, or protecting oneself from negative sexual experiences.
- Be informed about the laws in the region in which one lives, and the potential legal ramifications of violating them.
- Be aware of the resources available in case one needs them.

CHAPTER 30
A Final Note for Parents

There is a myth in this culture that this information needs to be shared in just the right way and at just the right time. Talking about sex with your kid is commonly referred to as having "The Talk."

But it is not a talk; it's a series of talks. As in, more than one.

As parents, we need to trust our judgment, our critical thinking, and our teaching abilities, just like we do with everything else. We help our kids create boundaries, grow, reinforce their decision-making skills, and start conversations about values.

When we leave them to their own resources, we leave gaps that will be filled by misinformed peers, pop culture, or the school system.

Here are the keys to talking to kids about sex:
- Make the subject a regular topic of conversation. It is not a onetime inoculation, it is a process.
- Find teachable moments and include sex whenever you talk about dating, love, drugs, friendship, health, media, and other related subjects. Do it every chance you get. Bringing it up at the dinner table may not be a good idea, but song lyrics, websites, movies, newscasts, and the like can be excellent opportunities for the topics to come up.
- Keep the lines of communication open. You'll need to discuss tough topics from time to time. If you and your teen are used to having conversations on a regular basis, even the awkward conversations will be easier. You don't want to think about them as sexually active creatures any more than they want to picture you as one. Sleep safe in the knowledge that even if your kids might be uncomfortable talking to you, they know they can.
- Respect your child's opinions. Enjoy the fact that your children are curious and have begun to think for themselves. Work to form a relationship with those opinions — even when they don't mesh with your own.
- If you cannot have the discussion with them, provide them with reliable and responsible alternatives, such as caring adults who can.
- Speak to your child's school about its sexual education curriculum, and don't assume that what your children are learning about sex outside your home is enough.

I wrote this book with the intention of providing information, education, and inspiration in order to contribute to healthy social and sexual relationships. As a parent myself, and as someone who has worked with teens for almost twenty years, I want to help others understand that concepts such as pregnancy, sexual identity, pornography, and even the word "sex" itself have very different meanings than they had when I began this work.

This book can be left in an accessible place, such as a bookshelf, desktop, coffee table, or waiting room of a health professional — somewhere low-key where a teen can discover it and read it in private. Parents can write notes in the margins and quietly leave it on an underager's nightstand, inviting them to ask questions, or they can read it chapter by chapter with their daughters, planning discussions afterward. Therapists and teachers can use it as an educational guideline for groups.

For the young people reading this, this book is designed to give you the tools and knowledge that you need to engage in sex and sexuality in a healthy way — having fun while doing as little harm to yourself and others as possible.

- Share the things you find in this book with friends and partners, in a "spread info, not chlamydia" kind of vibe.
- Read and revisit it as you grow and change as a sexual person.
- This book can also be used to help you open doors for discussion with your parents. Dog-ear a few specific pages or underline a random section with a highlighter and leave it out for them to find. They'll come to you.

I strongly encourage you to seek adult support and professional help if
- you are just becoming sexually active,
- your sexual behavior is causing problems in your life,
- your sexual behavior is causing problems in others' lives,
- you might be pregnant,
- you fear you have been exposed to infection,
- you have a history of abuse,
- you are afraid of your sexual or romantic partner,
- you have a history of self-harming behaviors,
- you have questions about your sexual identity,
- you feel unsupported or actively bullied because of your sexual identity.

This book is intended to provide information, education, and inspiration. It is intended to be an adjunct to, not a substitute for, professional medical advice. In addition, much of the information included here can and (most likely) will change with time and with the rapid development of technology, science, and culture.

I value feedback and questions, and I strive to respond. I can be reached via my website, *beheroes.net*.

Resources

ASSAULT AND ABUSE
Websites
National Youth Violence Prevention Center: *safeyouth.com*
Savvy Parents Safe Kids: *savvyparentssafekids.com*

Books
The Anger Workbook by Les Carter and Frank B. Minirth
The Gift of Fear and Other Survival Signals that Protect Us from Violence
   by Gavin de Becker

Phone
Gay & Transgender Hate Crime Hotline –1-800-616-HATE
National Runaway Hotline:1-800-231-6946
National Domestic Violence Hotline: 1-800-799-7233
National Youth Crisis Hotline: 1-800-448-HOPE (4663)
National Sexual Assault Hotline:1-800-656-HOPE (4663)
Stop It Now!: 1-888-773-8368
Teen Helpline: 1-800-400-0900

GLBTQ
Websites
American Psychological Association: *apa.org*
PFLAG (Parents, Families and Friends of Lesbians and Gays): *pflag.org*
Gay, Lesbian & Straight Education Network: *glsen.org*
Gay Teen Resources: *gayteenresources.org*
GLAAD (formerly the Gay and Lesbian Alliance Against Defamation): *glaad.org*
The Human Rights Campaign (HRC): *hrc.org*
The Intersex Society of North America: *isna.org*
The It Gets Better Project: *itgetsbetter.org*
Lambda Legal: *lambdalegal.org*
Tolerance.org

Books
GLBTQ: The Survival Guide for Queer and Questioning Teens by Kelly Huegel
*Always My Child: A Parent's Guide to Understanding Your Gay, Lesbian, Bisexual,
Transgendered, or Questioning Son or Daughter* by Kevin Jennings and Pat Shapiro

HEALTH AND HARM
Websites
Anorexia Nervosa and Related Eating Disorders: *anred.com*
Make Love, Not Porn: *makelovenotporn.com*
Through The Flame: *throughtheflame.org*

Books
In the Shadows of the Net by Patrick Carnes, David Delmonico and Elizabeth Griffin
My Body My Self by Lynda Madaras
Queen Bees and Wannabes by Rosalind Wiseman
The Wonder of Girls by Michael Gurian
Smart Girls' Guides (series) by Nancy Holyoke

Phone
Drug Help National Helplines: 1-800-378-4435
National Suicide Prevention Lifeline: 1-800-273-TALK (8255)
Eating Disorders Awareness and Prevention: 1-800-931-2237
Eating Disorders Center: 1-888-236-1188
Teenline: 1-800-522-TEEN (8336)
Center for the Prevention of School Violence: 1-800-299-6504
Gay, Lesbian, Bisexual, and Transgender (GLBT) Youth Support Line: 1-800-850-8078
Gay Men's Domestic Violence Project Crisis Hotline: 1-800-832-1901
Gay and Transgender Hate Crime Hotline: 1-800-616-HATE (4283)
National Adolescent Suicide Hotline: 1-800-621-4000
The Trevor Project: 1-866-488-7386

PREGNANCY
Websites
American Sexual Health Association: *ashastd.org*
Abortion Care Network:
abortioncarenetwork.org/resources/mom-dad/mom-dad-i-m-pregnant-for-young-people
National Abortion Federation: *prochoice.org*
National Campaign to Prevent Teen and Unplanned Pregnancy: *teenpregnancy.org*
National Right to Life: *nrlc.org*
Planned Parenthood: *plannedparenthood.org*

Phone
Emergency Contraception Information: 1-888-NOT-2-LATE
National Abortion Federation Hotline: 1-800-772-9100
Planned Parenthood: 1-800-230-PLAN (7526)
National Life Center pregnancy hotline: 1-800-848-LOVE (5683)

SEXUALITY
Websites
Advocates for Youth: *advocatesforyouth.org*
Be heroes: *beheroes.net*
Birds + Bees + Kids: *birdsandbeesandkids.com*
Go Ask Alice: *goaskalice.com*
The Guttmacher Institute: *guttmacher.org*
The Kaiser Family Foundation: *kff.org*
The Kinsey Institute: *kinseyinstitute.org*
KidsHealth: *kidshealth.org*
Hooking Up and Staying Hooked: *hookingupandstayinghooked.com*
Make Love, Not Porn: *makelovenotporn.com*
Scarleteen: *scarleteen.org*
Sex Ed Boot Camp: *sexedbootcamp.com*
Sexuality Information and Education Council of the United States: *siecus.org*
Talk with Your Kids: *talkwithyourkids.org*
teachingsexualhealth.ca
Teen Advice: *teenadvice.about.com*

Books
Dating Smarts - What Every Teen Needs to Date, Relate, or Wait! by Amy Lang
The Guide to Getting It On by Paul Joannides
S.E.X. by Heather Corinna
What's Happening to My Body? by Lynda Madaras and Area Anderson

Phone
Teen Helpline: 1-800-400-0900
Teenline: 1-800-522-TEEN (8336)

STIs
Websites
Centers for Disease Control and Prevention: *cdc.gov*
KidsHealth: *kidshealth.org*
Planned Parenthood: *plannedparenthood.org*
Teen Wire: *teenwire.org*

Phone
National Youth Crisis Hotline: 1-800-448-HOPE (4673)
Planned Parenthood: 1-800-230-PLAN (7526)
Teen Helpline: 1-800-400-0900
Teenline: 1-800-522-TEEN (8336)

References

Introduction
1. "Facts on American Teens' Sexual and Reproductive Health." Guttmacher Institute, accessed September 2008, *http://www.guttmacher.org/pubs/FB-ATSRH.html#n25.*
2. "U.S. Teen Sexual Activity." Kaiser Family Foundation, 2005, accessed March 2016, *http://enrichmentjournal.ag.org/200604/200604_4USTeenSexActi.pdf*
3. Ibid.
4. "Internet Crimes Against Children." Youth Internet Safety Survey, 2001, accessed July 2011, *http://www.ojp.usdoj.gov/ovc/publications/bulletins/internet_2_2001/internet_2_01_6.html.*
5. "Sex and Tech: Results from a Survey of Teens and Young Adults." The National Campaign to Prevent Teen and Unplanned Pregnancy, 2008, accessed December 2014, *http://thenationalcampaign.org/resource/sex-and-tech.*
6. "The Facts About Youth Sexual Abuse." The Advocacy Center, accessed February 21, 2014, *http://www.theadvocacycenter.org/adv_abuse.html.*
7. *Safe Practices for Motor Vehicle Operations.* 2006. American National Standards Institute/American Society of Safety Engineers, Des Plaines, Ill.

Chapter 2: Puberty
1. "Boys and Puberty." KidsHealth, accessed June 2011, *http://kidshealth.org/kid/grow/boy/boys_puberty.html.*
2. "Puberty 101 for Parents." Planned Parenthood, accessed February 2011, *http://www.plannedparenthood.org/parents/puberty-101-parents-22999.htm.*

Chapter 3: Body Issues and Body Image
1. "Puberty 101 for Parents." Planned Parenthood, accessed March 2011, *http://www.plannedparenthood.org/parents/puberty-101-parents-22999.htm.*
2. Todd, Nivin M.D., reviewer. "Menstrual Blood Problems." WebMD, September 29, 2014, accessed October 2015. *http://www.webmd.com/women/guide/menstrual-blood-problems-clots-color-and-thickness.*
3. Barcligt, Songhai, M.D. "Premenstrual Syndrome (PMS) Fact Sheet." 2010. Office of Women's Health, accessed July 2011, *http://www.womenshealth.gov/publications/our-publications/fact-sheet/premenstrual-syndrome.html.*
4. Kane, Jessica. "Here's How Much A Woman's Period Will Cost Her Over A Lifetime." The Huffington Post, May 18, 2015, accessed October 2015, *http://www.huffingtonpost.com/2015/05/18/period-cost-lifetime_n_7258780.html.*
5. "Toxic Shock Syndrome." The Mayo Clinic, accessed October 2015, *http://www.mayoclinic.org/diseases-conditions/toxic-shock-syndrome/basics/definition/con-20021326.*
6. Cottrell, B. H. "An updated review of evidence to discourage douching." MCN, *The American Journal of Maternal Child Nursing* 35 (2) (March–April 2010): 102–7; quiz 108–9.
7. "Curtains for semi-nude justice statue." BBC News, last modified January 29, 2002, accessed May 2011, *http://news.bbc.co.uk/2/hi/1788845.stm.*
8. "Breast Implants Linked with Suicide." Reuters, last modified August 9, 2007, *http://www.reuters.com/article/us-implants-suicide-idUSN0836919020070809.*
9. "Breast Self-Exams." Johns Hopkins Medical Center, Breast Center, accessed November 2015, *http://www.hopkinsmedicine.org/breast_center/treatments_services/breast_cancer_screening/breast_self_exam.html.*
10. "Symptoms and Signs." National Breast Cancer Foundation, accessed November 2015, *http://www.nationalbreastcancer.org/breast-cancer-symptoms-and-signs.*
11. "The initial reproductive health visit." American College of Obstetricians and Gynecologists, Committee on Adolescent Health, Opinion No. 460. Obstetrics and Gynecology 2010: 240–3.

12. Herbenick, Debby Ph.D., MPH. "Erect Penile Length and Circumference Dimensions of 1,661 Sexually Active Men in the United States." *The Journal of Sexual Medicine*, 11 (January 2014): 93–101. Article first published online: July 10, 2013.

13. Zimmerman, Mike. "15 Facts You Didn't Know About Your Penis." Men's Health, accessed July 2011, *http://www.menshealth.com/mhlists/penis_facts/Penis_Fact_9.php*.

14. Veale, David, Sarah Miles, Sally Bramley, Gordon Muir, and John Hodsoll. "Am I normal? A systematic review and construction of nomograms for flaccid and erect penis length and circumference in up to 15 521 men." BJU International. Wiley Online Library, accessed September 2015, *http://onlinelibrary.wiley.com/doi/10.1111/bju.13010/full*

15. "Alice" (a team of Columbia University health educators, health care providers, other health professionals, and information and research specialists and writers). 2002. "How deep is the average vagina, and does it elongate when something's in it?" "Go Ask Alice!" Columbia University, accessed August 2011, *http://www.goaskalice.columbia.edu/answered-questions/how-deep-average-vagina-and-does-it-elongate-when-somethings-it*.

16. Dave, S., A.M. Johnson, K.A. Fenton, C.H. Mercer, B. Erens, K. Wellings. 2003. "Male circumcision in Britain: findings from a national probability sample survey." *Sexually Transmitted Infections* 79: 499–500.

17. "Eating Disorder Statistics." South Carolina Department of Mental Health, 2006, accessed February 2011, *http://www.state.sc.us/dmh/anorexia/statistics.htm*.

18. Ibid. Accessed May 2011.

19. Ibid.

Chapter 4: Sex, Gender, and Orientation

1. Gates, Gary J. "How Many People Are Lesbian, Gay Bisexual and Transgender?" The Williams Institute at UCLA School of Law, April 2011, accessed April 2014, *http://williamsinstitute.law.ucla.edu/research/census-lgbt-demographics-studies/how-many-people-are-lesbian-gay-bisexual-and-transgender*.

2. "1,500 Animal Species Practice Homosexuality." News Medical, 2006, accessed September 2011, *http://www.news-medical.net/news/2006/10/23/1500-animal-species-practice-homosexuality.aspx*.

3. Gates, Gary J. "How Many People Are Lesbian, Gay Bisexual and Transgender?" The Williams Institute at UCLA School of Law, April 2011, accessed April 2011, *http://williamsinstitute.law.ucla.edu/research/census-lgbt-demographics-studies/how-many-people-are-lesbian-gay-bisexual-and-transgender*.

4. "A Survey of LGBT Americans." Pew Research Center, June 13, 2013, *http://www.pewsocialtrends.org/2013/06/13/a-survey-of-lgbt-americans*.

5. Kinsey's Heterosexual-Homosexual Rating Scale. The Kinsey Institute, 2009, accessed September 2011, *http://www.iub.edu/~kinsey/research/ak-hhscale.html*.

6. Robinson, B. A.. 2006. "Reparative Therapy: Statements by Professional Associations and Their Leaders." Religious Tolerance, accessed June 2011, *http://religioustolerance.org/hom_prof3.htm*.

7. "Homosexual Behavior Due to Genetics and Environmental Factors." Biology News Net, 2008, accessed June 2011, *http://www.biologynews.net/archives/2008/06/29/homosexual_behavior_due_to_genetics_and_environmental_factors.html*.

8. "Be Yourself: Questions and Answers for Gay, Lesbian and Bisexual Youth." Lambda, 1994, accessed March 2016, *http://seattle-pflag.org/pflag/wp-content/uploads/2015/03/Be-Yourself.pdf*.

9. "Gay, Lesbian, Bisexual, and Transgender (GLBT) Rights Fact Sheet." Parents and Friends of Lesbians and Gays (PFLAG), 2008, accessed June 2011, *http://community.pflag.org/page.aspx?pid=442*.

10. Remafedi, Gary, M.D., MPH, James A. Farrow, M.D., and Robert W. Deisher, M.D. "Risk factors for attempted suicide in gay and bisexual youth." *Pediatrics* 87 (1991): 869–875.

11. R. L. Spitzer. "The diagnostic status of homosexuality in DSM-III: a reformulation of the issues." *American Journal of Psychiatry* 138 (1981): 210–215.

12. "Matthew Shepard and James Byrd, Jr. Hate Crimes Prevention Act." Human Rights Campaign, last modified February 1, 2010, accessed November 2011, *http://www.hrc.org/resources/entry/questions-and-answers-the-matthew-shepard-and-james-byrd-jr.-hate-crimes-pr.*
13. "Therapies Focused on Attempts to Change Sexual Orientation." American Psychiatric Association Assembly position statement. American Psychiatric Association, 2000, accessed August 2011, *http://www.psychiatry.org/File%20Library/Learn/Archives/Position-2000-Therapies-Change-Sexual-Orientation.pdf.*
14. "Tips for Allies of Transgender People." GLAAD, accessed April 2014, *http://www.glaad.org/transgender/allies.*

Chapter 6: Sexual Arousal
1. Ybarra, Michele Ph.D., MPH, Dorothy L. Espelage, Ph.D., Jennifer Langhinrichsen-Rohling, Ph.D., Josephine D. Korchmaros, Ph.D., and Danah Boyd, Ph.D. "National Rates of Adolescent Physical, Psychological, and Sexual Teen-Dating Violence." American Psychological Association, July 2013, accessed November 2015, *http://www.apa.org/news/press/releases/2013/07/dating-violence.aspx.*
2. "Factsheets: Teen Dating Violence," National Victim Center, accessed November 2015, *http://www.svfreenyc.org/survivors_factsheet_48.html.*
3. Ibid.
4. Masters, William H. and Virginia Johnson. *Human Sexual Response.* (New York: Bantam, 1981), adaptation.
5. Dan Savage. "Savage Love: Play with Her Clit." *The Stranger,* July 19, 2007.
6. Franklin Lowe, M.D., MPH, FACS. "All About Semen." *Menstuff,* 2006, accessed July 2011, *http://www.menstuff.org/issues/byissue/semen.html.*

Chapter 7: Sexual Activity
1. "Human Sexual Behavior." *The Journal of Evolutionary Philosophy,* accessed August 2011, *http://www.evolutionary-philosophy.net/human_sexuality.html.*
2. Gerressu, M., C. H. Mercer, C. A. Graham, K. Wellings, A. M. Johnson. "Prevalence of masturbation and associated factors in a British national probability survey." *Archives of Sexual Behavior* 37, no. 2 (April 2008): 266–78.
3. Haeberle, Edwin, Ph.D. *The Sex Atlas.* New York: The Continuum Publishing Company, 1983.
4. "Alice" (a team of Columbia University health educators, health care providers, other health professionals, and information and research specialists and writers). 1995. "Masturbation Healthy?" Go Ask Alice! Columbia University, accessed February 2011, *http://www.goaskalice.columbia.edu/answered-questions/masturbation-healthy.*
5. "Phthalates." Tox Town, U.S. National Library of Medicine. Last updated May 13, 2015, accessed, November 2015, *https://toxtown.nlm.nih.gov/text_version/chemicals.php?id=24.*
6. Ropelato, Jerry. "Internet Pornography Statistics." Top Ten Reviews, 2006, accessed August 2011, *http://internet-filter-review.toptenreviews.com/internet-pornography-statistics.html.*
7. Case, William. *The Art of Kissing.* 2nd ed. (New York, New York: St. Martin's Griffin, 1995).
8. Güntürkün, Onur. "Adult persistence of head-turning asymmetry." *Nature,* 421, 711 (February 13, 2003).

Chapter 9: Vaginal Sex
1. "Female Orgasm." The Medical Center for Female Sexuality, accessed April 2011, *http://www.centerforfemalesexuality.com/orgasm.htm.*

Chapter 10: Anal Sex
1. Savage, Dan. "Savage Love: Wiggle Room." *The Stranger,* February 25, 2010.
2. Em & Lo. "The Bottom Line." *New York Magazine,* October 25, 2007.
3. "Increase in Anal Intercourse Involving At-risk Teens and Young Adults." Medical News Today, last updated November 22, 2008, accessed January 2011,

http://www.medicalnewstoday.com/releases/130181.php.
4. Savage, Dan. "Savage Love: Saddlebacked!" *The Stranger*, January 29, 2009.
5. Brent, Bill. *The Ultimate Guide to Anal Sex for Men* (San Francisco: Cleis Press, 2002).
6. "HIV Transmission." Divisions of HIV/AIDS Prevention, National Center for HIV/AIDS, Viral Hepatitis, STD, and TB Prevention, 2010, accessed March 2011, *http://www.cdc.gov/hiv/resources/qa/transmission.htm.*
7. Saletan, William. "Ass Backwards: The media's silence about rampant anal sex." *Slate*, posted Sept. 20, 2005, *http://www.slate.com/id/2126643.*
8. Boonstra, Heather. 2005. "Condoms, Contraceptives and Nonoxynol-9: Complex Issues Obscured by Ideology." *The Guttmacher Report on Public Policy* 8, no. 2 (May 2005): 4–6, 16.

Chapter 11: Abstinence and Virginity
1. Tedeschi Sara K., B.A., Loida E. Bonney, M.D., MPH, Rosario Manalo, M.D., Kenneth H. Mayer, M.D., Susan Shepardson, M.A., Josiah D. Rich, M.D., MPH, Michelle A. Lally, M.D., MSc. 2007. "Vaccination in Juvenile Correctional Facilities: State Practices, Hepatitis B, and the Impact on Anticipated Sexually Transmitted Infection Vaccines." *Public Health Reports* 122, no.1, (January–February 2007): 44–48.
2. "'Virginity Pledges' by Adolescents May Bias Their Reports of Premarital Sex." Harvard School of Public Health, press release, May 2, 2006, accessed June 2011, *http://www.hsph.harvard.edu/news/press-releases/2006-releases/press05022006.html.*
3. "Comparing effectiveness of birth control methods." Planned Parenthood (adapted from World Health Organization, 2007), accessed December 2010, *http://www.plannedparenthood.org/health-topics/birth-control/birth-control-effectiveness-chart-22710.htm.*

Chapter 13: Sexually Transmitted Infections (STIs)
1. "Sexually Transmitted Diseases (STDs)." Planned Parenthood, 2011, accessed June 2011, *http://www.plannedparenthood.org/health-topics/stds-hiv-safer-sex-101.htm.*
2. "STD Awareness Month Facts." Minnesota Department of Health, 2011, accessed April 2011, *http://www.health.state.mn.us/divs/idepc/dtopics/stds/stdbasics.html.*
3. "STDs in America: How Many Cases and at What Cost?" American Social Health Association/Kaiser Family Foundation, 1998, accessed March 2016, *http://kff.org/hivaids/sexually-transmitted-diseases-in-america-how-many/.*
4. "11 Facts About Teens and STIs." *DoSomething.org*, accessed June 2011, *http://www.dosomething.org/tipsandtools/11-facts-about-teens-and-stds.*
5. "STDs in Adolescents and Young Adults." Centers for Disease Control and Prevention, 2010, accessed December 2010, *http://www.cdc.gov/std/stats09/adol.htm.*
6. "Gonorrhea Gonococcal Infection." New York State Department of Health, 2006, accessed November 2010, *http://www.health.ny.gov/diseases/communicable/gonorrhea/fact_sheet.htm.*
7. "Gonorrhea – CDC Fact Sheet." Centers for Disease Control and Prevention, 2011, *http://www.cdc.gov/std/gonorrhea/stdfact-gonorrhea.htm.*
8. Cullins, Vanessa, M.D. "Chlamydia." Planned Parenthood, updated 2011, accessed June 2011, *http://www.plannedparenthood.org/health-info/stds-hiv-safer-sex/chlamydia.*
9. "Reported Cases of Sexually Transmitted Diseases on the Rise, Some at Alarming Rate." NCHHSTP Newsroom, Centers for Disease Control and Prevention, November 17, 2015, accessed November 2015, *http://www.cdc.gov/nchhstp/newsroom/2015/std-surveillance-report-press-release.html.*
10. Ibid.
11. Ibid.
12. "Genital Herpes Statistics." Herpes Clinic, accessed March 2016, *http://www.herpesclinic.com/genitalherpes/genitalherpesstatistics/.*

13. "The ABCs of Viral Hepatitis." Centers for Disease Control and Prevention, 2011, accessed August 2011, *http://www.cdc.gov/Features/ViralHepatitis.*

14. Ibid.
15. "Hepatitis B Vaccine (Recombinant)." Merck and Co. Inc., 2011, accessed July 2011, *http://www.merck.com/product/usa/pi_circulars/r/recombivax_hb/recombivax_pi.pdf*
16. Simon, Harvey, M.D., Harvard Medical School. "Hepatitis B." *The New York Times*, 2011, accessed September 2011, *http://health.nytimes.com/health/guides/disease/rubella/hepatitis-b.html*.
17. "Hepatitis B Foundation Participates in U.S. Capitol Briefing." Hepatitis B Foundation, 2005, accessed July 2011, *http://www.hepb.org/pdf/Capitol_Briefing7_05.pdf*.
18. "Information About Gardasil." *Gardasil.com*, 2011, accessed August 2011, *http://www.gardasil.com*.
19. "Study: Half of Men May Be Infected with HPV." The Huffington Post, 2011, accessed March 2011, *http://www.huffingtonpost.com/2011/02/28/half-men-infected-hpv_n_829449.html*.

Chapter 14: HIV/AIDS 101
1. "U.S. Teen Sexual Activity." Kaiser Family Foundation, 2005, accessed January 2011, *http://kff.org/womens-health-policy/fact-sheet/sexual-health-of-adolescents-and-young-adults-in-the-united-states*.
2. "Condoms and STDs." Centers for Disease Control and Prevention, 2014, accessed December 2014, *http://www.cdc.gov/condomeffectiveness/docs/condoms_and_stds.pdf*.
3. Truvada website, *http://www.truvada.com*.
4. McCullom, Rod. "Lowering the Age for HIV Prevention." *The Atlantic*, February 11, 2015, accessed November 2015, *http://www.theatlantic.com/health/archive/2015/02/lowering-the-age-for-hiv-prevention/385303/*.
5. Grant, R. M. , J. R. Lama, P. L. Anderson, et al.: iPrEx Study Team. "Preexposure chemoprophylaxis for HIV prevention in men who have sex with men." *New England Journal of Medicine*, 363, 27 (2010): 2587–99. Accessed November 2015, *http://www.nejm.org/doi/full/10.1056/NEJMoa1011205*.
6. "Lower Your Sexual Risk for HIV." *AIDS.gov*, accessed November 2015, *https://www.aids.gov/hiv-aids-basics/prevention/reduce-your-risk/sexual-risk-factors/*.

Chapter 15: Contraception and Safer Sex
1. Harlap, S., K. Kost, and J. D. Forrest. *Preventing Pregnancy, Protecting Health: A New Look at Birth Control Choices in the United States* (New York, New York: The Alan Guttmacher Institute, 1991).
2. "Abstinence." Klickitat County Public Health, 2006, accessed February 2011, *http://www.klickitatcounty.org/health/Content.asp?fC=168&fD=45*.
3. "Comparing effectiveness of birth control methods." Planned Parenthood (adapted from World Health Organization 2007), accessed December 2010, *http://www.plannedparenthood.org/health-topics/birth-control/birth-control-effectiveness-chart-22710.htm*.
4.-9. Ibid.
10. Cullins, Vanessa, M.D., MPH, MBA. "Condom." Planned Parenthood, 2011, *http://www.plannedparenthood.org/health-topics/birth-control/condom-10187.htm*.
11. Frezieres, R. G., T. L. Walsh, A. L. Nelson, V. A. Clark, A. H. Coulson. "Breakage and acceptability of a polyurethane condom: A randomized, controlled study." *Family Planning Perspectives* 10 (January 24, 2005). *http://www.niaid.nih.gov/dmid/stds/condomreport.pdf*.
12. Davis, K., C. A. Stappenbeck, J. Norris, W. H. George, , A. J. Jacques-Tiura, T. J. Schraufnagel, and K. F. Kajumulo. "Young men's condom use resistance tactics: A latent profile analysis." *Journal of Sex Research* 51, no. 4.
13.-20. Ibid.
21. Zibners, A., B. A. Cromer, J. Hayes. "Comparison of continuation rates for hormonal contraception among adolescents." *Journal of Pediatric and Adolescent Gynecology* 12 (1999): 90–4. *http://www.ncbi.nlm.nih.gov/pubmed/10326194*.
22. Raine, T. R., A. Foster-Rosales, U. D. Upadhyay, et al. "One-year contraceptive continuation and pregnancy in adolescent girls and women initiating hormonal

contraceptives." *Obstetrics & Gynecology* 117 (February 2011): 363–71. *http://www.ncbi.nlm.nih.gov/pubmed/21252751.*

23. "Plan B: The New Morning After Pill." Estronaut, A Forum for Women's Health, 1999, accessed 2011, *http://www.estronaut.com/a/Plan_B_Morning_After_Emergecy_Contraceptive.htm.*

24. "Comparing effectiveness of birth control methods." Planned Parenthood (adapted from World Health Organization 2007), accessed December 2010, *http://www.plannedparenthood. org/health-topics/birth-control/birth-control-effectiveness-chart-22710.htm.*

25. Ibid.

26. Zernike, Kate. "Use of Contraception Drops, Slowing Decline of Abortion Rate." *The New York Times*, May 5, 2006, accessed May 2011, *http://www.nytimes.com/2006/05/05/health/05abort.html.*

27. Robinson, B. A. "Major U.S. Laws Concerning Abortion." Religious Tolerance, 2008, accessed January 2011, *http://www.religioustolerance.org/abo_supr.htm.*

28. "Plan B: The New Morning After Pill." Estronaut, A Forum for Women's Health, 1999, accessed 2011, *http://www.estronaut.com/a/Plan_B_Morning_After_Emergecy_Contraceptive.htm.*

Chapter 18: Sexual Abuse and Assault

1. Van Dam, Carla, Ph.D. *Identifying Child Molesters* (New York, New York: Haworth Maltreatment and Trauma Press, 2001), p. 50.

2. Maltz, Wendy. *The Sexual Healing Journey: A Guide for Survivors of Sexual Abuse* (New York, New York: HarperCollins, 2001), p. 30.

3. "Statistics." National Center for Missing and Exploited Children, 2009, accessed August 2011, *http://www.missingkids.com/missingkids/servlet/PageServlet?LanguageCountry=en_ US&PageId=2810.*

4. Snyder, Howard. *Sexual Assault of Young Children as Reported to Law Enforcement: Victim, Incident, and Offender Characteristics*: "Table 1: Age Profile of the Victims of Sexual Assault." U.S. Department of Justice, Bureau of Justice Statistics, 2000.

5. Black, Michelle Lynberg, Ph.D., MPH. "The National Intimate Partner and Sexual Violence Survey." Centers for Disease Control and Prevention, National Center for Injury Prevention and Control, Division of Violence Prevention, April 2011, accessed December 2015, *http://vawnet.org/Assoc_Files_VAWnet/NRCWebinar_NISVSBriefingHandout.pdf.*

6. Koss, Mary and Mary Harvey. *The Rape Victim: Clinical and Community Interventions* (Newbury Park, California: Sage Library of Social Research, 1991).

Chapter 19: Personal Safety

1. "Statistics." *RAINN.org*, accessed March 2016, *https://rainn.org/statistics*

2. Weiss, Susan. "Date Rape Drugs Fact Sheet." The Department of Health and Human Services Office on Women's Health, accessed August 2011, *http://womenshealth.gov/publications/our-publications/fact-sheet/date-rape-drugs.html.*

Chapter 20: Exposure and Exploitation

1. "Youth Internet Safety Survey." Internet Crimes Against Children, 2001, accessed July 2011, *http://www.ojp.usdoj.gov/ovc/publications/bulletins/internet_2_2001/internet_2_01_6.html.*

2. De Becker, Gavin. *The Gift of Fear* (New York, New York: Dell Publishing, 1997).

3. Henry, Shawn. "Shawn Henry on Cyber Safety." Federal Bureau of Investigation, April 2014, *http://www.fbi.gov/news/videos/henry_051611.*

4. "Media and Children." American Academy of Pediatrics, April 2014, *http://www.aap.org/en-us/advocacy-and-policy/aap-health-initiatives/pages/media-and-children.aspx.*

5. "ESRB Ratings Guide." Entertainment Software Rating Board, April 2014, *http://www.esrb.org/ratings/principles_guidelines.jsp.*

6. Clawson, Heather J., Nicole Dutch, Amy Solomon and Lisa Goldblatt-Grace. "Human Trafficking Into and Within the United States: A Review of the Literature." Office of the

Assistant Secretary for Planning and Evaluation, U.S. Department of Health and Social Services, accessed November 2015, *http://aspe.hhs.gov/basic-report/human-trafficking-and-within-united-states-review-literature.*

7. Bales, Kevin. "The Number." The CNN Freedom Project Ending Modern Day Slavery, accessed November 2015, *http://thecnnfreedomproject.blogs.cnn.com/category/the-facts/the-number.*

8. Clawson, Heather J., Nicole Dutch, Amy Solomon and Lisa Goldblatt-Grace. "Human Trafficking Into and Within the United States: A Review of the Literature." Office of the Assistant Secretary for Planning and Evaluation, U.S. Department of Health and Social Services, accessed November 2015, *http://aspe.hhs.gov/basic-report/human-trafficking-and-within-united-states-review-literature.*

Chapter 21: Porn

1. Bev Betkowski, "Rural teen boys most likely to access pornography, study shows," Faculty News, University of Alberta, accessed March 2016, *www.eurekalert.org/pub_releases/2007-02/uoa-oit022307.php*

2. "Online Safety Statistics." My Internet Safety Coach, 2009, accessed December 2010, *http://myinternetsafetycoach.com/?p=18.*

3. Ropelato, Jerry. "Internet Pornography Statistics." TopTenReviews, 2006, accessed August 2011, *http://internet-filter-review.toptenreviews.com/internet-pornography-statistics.html.*

4. Zimbardo, Phillip. "The Demise of Guys?" TED Talks, video, 4:46 minutes, March 2011, accessed August 2011, *http://www.ted.com/talks/zimchallenge?language=en.*

5. Wilson, Gary. "The Great Porn Experiment." TEDx Glasgow, video, 16:28 minutes, May 16, 2012, *https://www.youtube.com/watch?v=wSF82AwSDiU.*

6. Ibid.

Chapter 23: Sexting

1. Ahmed, Murad. "Teen 'Sexting' Craze Leading to Child Porn Arrests in U.S." *The Times* (London), January 14, 2009.

2. "Sexual Offenses: Federal Law 18 U.S.C. 1466A – Obscene Visual Representations of the Sexual Abuse of Children." *SexLaws.org*, accessed March 2016, *https://www.law.cornell.edu/uscode/text/18/1466A*

Chapter 24: Cyberbullying

1. "Cyberbullying." *Trends & Tudes*, April 2007 (vol. 6, issue 4), HarrisInteractive, *http://www.ncpc.org/resources/files/pdf/bullying/Cyberbullying%20Trends%20-%20Tudes.pdf.*

2. Benaroch, Roy, M.D. "Preventing Teen Suicide," *WebMD.com*, February 3, 2012, *http://teens.webmd.com/preventing-teen-suicide.*

3. Van Geel, Mitch, Ph.D., Paul Vedder, Ph.D., Jenny Tanilon, Ph.D. "Relationship between peer victimization, cyberbullying, and suicide in children and adolescents: a meta-analysis." *JAMA Pediatrics* 168, no. 5: 435–42. Published online March 10, 2014, *http://www.ncbi.nlm.nih.gov/pubmed/24615300.*

4. "Teens, kindness and cruelty on social network sites." Pew Research Center, Family Online Safety Institute, Cable in the Classroom, November 9, 2011, *http://www.pewinternet.org/2011/11/09/teens-kindness-and-cruelty-on-social-network-sites-2.*

5. "Teen Online and Wireless Safety Survey: Cyberbullying, Sexting and Parental Controls." Cox Communications, in partnership with the National Center for Missing and Exploited Children, May 2009, *http://www.cox.com/wcm/en/aboutus/datasheet/takecharge/2009-teen-survey.pdf.*

6. Bowman, Darcia Harris. "Survey of Students Documents the Extent of Bullying." Education Week, May 2, 2001, *http://www.edweek.org/ew/articles/2001/05/02/33bully.h20.html.*

Chapter 25: Online Gaming

1. Duggan, Maeve. "Online Harassment: Summary of Findings." Pew Research Center,

accessed October 2015, *http://www.pewinternet.org/2014/10/22/online-harassment/*.
2. "Study Finds Female-Name Chat Users Get 25 Times More Malicious Messages."
University of Maryland, A. James Clark School of Engineering May 2006, accessed November
2015, *http://ece.umd.edu/news/news_story.php?id=1788*.

Chapter 26: The Statistical Reality
1. Warner, Jennifer. "Premarital Sex the Norm in America." *WebMD Health News*, December 6,
2001, accessed March 2011, *http://www.webmd.com/sex-relationships/news/20061220/premari-tal-sex-the-norm-in-america*.
2. *Public Health Reports*, 122, no. 1 (January–February 2007): 73–8.
3. "The History of Federal Abstinence-Only Funding." Advocates for Youth, accessed July
2011, *http://www.advocatesforyouth.org/publications/429?task=view*.
4. Trenholm, Christopher, Barbara Devaney, Ken Fortson, Lisa Quay, Justin Wheeler, Melissa
Clark. "Impacts of Four Title V, Section 510 Abstinence Education Programs." Mathematica
Policy Research Inc., April 2007, accessed April 2011, *http://www.mathematica-mpr.com/publications/pdfs/impactabstinence.pdf*.
5. "Facts on American Teens' Sexual and Reproductive Health." Guttmacher Institute, May
2004, accessed September 2011, *http://www.guttmacher.org/pubs/FB-ATSRH.html#n25*.
6. Kaper, Kidder, host. "Sex Education in America." *Sex Is Fun*, no. 116, April 10, 2008, *http://sif101-200.sexisfun.net/search?updated-max=2008-04-29T13%3A17%3A00-07%3A00&max-results=150*.

Chapter 27: The 'Gay' Issue (That Impacts the Straight Kids, Too)
1. Lee, Carol. "Gay Teens Ignored by High School Sex Ed Classes." Women's eNews, February
10, 2002, *http://womensenews.org/2002/02/gay-teens-ignored-high-school-sex-ed-classes*.
2. James, Susan Donaldson. "Study Reports Anal Sex on Rise Among Teens." ABC News,
December 10, 2008, *http://abcnews.go.com/Health/story?id=6428003*.
3. Saletan, William. "Ass Backwards: The media's silence about rampant anal sex." *Slate*,
September 20, 2005, accessed October 2011, *http://www.slate.com/id/2126643*.
4. "Sexual Health Statistics for Teenagers and Young Adults in the United States." Kaiser
Family Foundation, accessed September 2011, *http://www.kff.org/womenshealth/upload/3040-03.pdf*.
5. "State Policies in Brief: Sex and HIV Education." Guttmacher Institute, last modified
December 1, 2014, accessed August 2011, *http://www.guttmacher.org/statecenter/spibs/spib_SEpdf*.
6. Russell, S. T. and K. Joyner. "Adolescent sexual orientation and suicide risk: evidence from
a national study." *American Journal of Public Health* 91, no. 8 (August 2001): 1276–81.
7. Hubbard, Jeremy. "The Conversation: It Gets Better Project." ABC News, September 30,
2010. *http://abcnews.go.com/WN/dan-savage-project-world-news-conversation/story?id=11764984*.

Chapter 28: Abstinence-Only Education versus Comprehensive Sex Education
1. Trenholm, Christopher, Barbara Devaney, Ken Fortson, Lisa Quay, Justin Wheeler, Melissa
Clark. "Impacts of Four Title V, Section 510 Abstinence Education Programs." Mathematica
Policy Research Inc., April 2007, accessed April 2011, *http://www.mathematica-mpr.com/publications/pdfs/impactabstinence.pdf*.
2. Kohler, Pamela K., R.N., MPH, Lisa E. Manhart, Ph.D., and William E. Lafferty, M.D.
"Abstinence-Only and Comprehensive Sex Education and the Initiation of Sexual Activity and
Teen Pregnancy." *Journal of Adolescent Health*, 42 no. 4 (April 2008): 344–351.
http://www.jahonline.org/article/S1054-139X%2807%2900426-0/abstract.
3. McKeon, Brigid. "Effective Sex Education." Advocates for Youth, 2006, accessed October
2011, *http://www.advocatesforyouth.org/publications/450?task=view*.

Index

ABOUT PARENTMAP

ParentMap is a media company that inspires, supports, and connects a growing community of wise-minded parents by publishing intelligent, trusted, and thought-leading content to equip them for their essential role as their child's first and most important teacher. ParentMap's unique social-venture business model drives its vision and day-to-day operations, ensuring that publication readers and website visitors are given the most current information related to early learning, child health and development, and parenting. In all of its work and through all of its resources and publishing channels, ParentMap is dedicated to providing outstanding editorial content, advocating for children and families, and contributing to community.

Visit us at *parentmap.com*.

Other ParentMap titles:

Spare Me 'The Talk'!: A Guy's Guide to Sex, Relationships, and Growing Up
By Jo Langford, M.A.

Getting to Calm, The Early Years: Cool-Headed Strategies for Raising Happy, Caring, and Independent Three- to Seven-Year-Olds
By Laura S. Kastner, Ph.D.

Wise-Minded Parenting: 7 Essentials for Raising Successful Tweens and Teens
By Laura S. Kastner, Ph.D. with Kristen A. Russell

Getting to Calm: Cool Headed Strategies for Parenting Tweens and Teens
By Laura S. Kastner, Ph.D., and Jennifer Wyatt

Beyond Smart: Boosting Your Child's Social, Emotional, and Academic Potential
By Linda Morgan

Northwest Kid Trips
By Lora Shinn

ParentMap books are available at special discounts when purchased in bulk for premiums and sales promotions, as well as for fundraisers or educational use. Contact *books@parentmap.com* for more information.

ABOUT THE AUTHOR

Jo Langford is a parent, sex educator, and master-level therapist who has worked for two decades with youths in high schools, and residential, medical, and psychiatric settings.

Jo uses information, education, and humor to help families increase their knowledge and self-confidence as a proactive defense against the unfortunate consequences that sometimes accompany teen sexual behavior.

He has spent the past 15 years in private practice, which centers on that intersection of youth, sexuality, technology, and behavior, providing therapy to adolescents regarding sexuality issues as well as comprehensive sexuality education for teens and their families.

He is a certified counselor and treatment provider in Washington state as well as a member of the human sexuality faculty for Saybrook University.

He can often be found writing in cool, hipster coffeehouses around Seattle (or binge-watching something on Netflix). Schedule Jo for your next speaking engagement; and learn more about him and his work with youths, parents, agencies, and professionals to promote healthy, positive, and safe sexual and social behavior at his website, *BeHeroes.net*.